Two-of-a-Kind Quilts

12 SCRAPPY DESIGNS THAT ARE DOUBLE THE FUN

Lissa Alexander and Susan Ache

Martingale®
Create with Confidence

Two-of-a-Kind Quilts:
12 Scrappy Designs That Are Double the Fun
© 2022 by Lissa Alexander and Susan Ache

Martingale®
18939 120th Ave NE, Suite 101
Bothell, WA 98011-9511 USA
ShopMartingale.com

Printed in Hong Kong
27 26 25 24 23 22   8 7 6 5 4 3 2 1

Library of Congress Cataloging-in-Publication Data is available upon request.

ISBN: 978-1-68356-210-8

MISSION STATEMENT

We empower makers who use fabric and yarn to make life more enjoyable.

CREDITS

PRESIDENT AND CHIEF VISIONARY OFFICER
Jennifer Erbe Keltner

CONTENT DIRECTOR
Karen Costello Soltys

DESIGN MANAGER
Adrienne Smitke

TECHNICAL EDITOR
Elizabeth Tisinger Beese

PRODUCTION MANAGER
Regina Girard

COPY EDITOR
Melissa Bryan

PHOTOGRAPHER
Adam Albright
Brent Kane

ILLUSTRATOR
Sandy Loi

SPECIAL THANKS
Photography for this book was taken at:
Carol Hansen's the Garden Barn in Indianola, Iowa
The home of Samantha Keltner of Des Moines, Iowa
The home of Julie Smiley of Des Moines, Iowa

Contents

Double the Scrappy Fun 4
Meet our Machine Quilters 7

TWO OF A KIND
Daisy Squared by Susan Ache 11
One by Two by Lissa Alexander 21

PICK A MIX
American Pavement by Lissa Alexander 29
Ruffled Hibiscus by Susan Ache 37

TWO HALVES OF A WHOLE
Windjammer by Susan Ache 47
Sunshine Day by Lissa Alexander 59

SCRAPS GONE WILD
Big Wreaths by Lissa Alexander 71
Safety First by Susan Ache 79

A TALE OF TWO SEASONS
Spooky Waves by Susan Ache 87
Mistletoe by Lissa Alexander 97

I'LL HAVE SECONDS
Garden Path by Lissa Alexander 105
Roundel by Susan Ache 115

A Big Finish 126
About the Authors 128

Double the Scrappy Fun!

When we set out to write a book about how we make scrap quilts—how we choose fabrics, what might inspire the design, and so forth—we thought it would be fun to challenge ourselves with categories of quilts. The quilts you see in this book are the result. We came up with six concepts or categories, and from there we each did our own thing. We didn't share notes or talk about what blocks we were using; we simply came up with our own takes on what each concept meant to us. So, you may look at the two quilts in the same category and wonder how they're related. All we can say is that they are *loosely* tied together by our themes!

Don't worry; we won't make you guess the themes. We think that in addition to making the patterns in this book, you, too, might be inspired to create your own version or your own unique quilt in any of these categories. We dare you—it's great fun! So without further ado, here's where we started:

TWO OF A KIND. Here, we each picked two things that go together as terrifically as peanut butter and jelly or salt and pepper. What did we choose? Upon a quick perusal of her stash, Susan worked with dots and stripes. Lissa sorted through her leftover strips from Jelly Rolls and Honey Buns, and the challenge was on!

PICK A MIX. Two-color quilts are perennial favorites. But often, one of the two colors is white. Think classic red-and-white or blue-and-white quilts. Instead, we went for two colors that don't need white to be great together. We'll show you how you can make the most of just two colors by using all the shades, tints, and tones of each color to get a big bang for your buck.

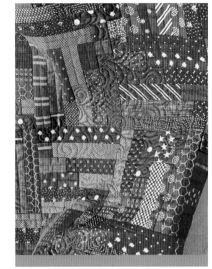

TWO HALVES OF A WHOLE. For this idea, we split the color wheel down the middle and each picked a half. Susan opted for cool beachy colors, while Lissa worked with her favorite hot yellows, oranges, corals, and reds. Which half would you choose? Are you a water baby? Or a sun seeker?

A TALE OF TWO SEASONS. Make a scrap quilt that reflects your favorite holiday or season. Susan chose Halloween; Lissa picked Christmas. Unbeknownst to one another, we both ended up designing a riff on a traditional Ocean Waves pattern. (Can you spot the difference? Hint, squares vs. triangles.)

SCRAPS GONE WILD. What can we say? The more fabrics, the merrier! But to make things easy—for us *and* for you—we limited the patchwork pieces to squares and rectangles. There's not a triangle to be found! If you'd like to be scrappy, but think you're not, dip your toe in the water with Susan's controlled scrappy color palette.

I'LL HAVE SECONDS. We know quilters love it when they put their blocks together and a secondary design emerges. Not only are the results stunning, but piecing the quilt is also so much easier than you'd think. Whether you use an alternate block or opt for clever sashing, we're sure you'll agree that you want seconds too!

Thanks for joining us on what's been a fun and exciting journey into using our scraps and our stashes. We hope that you enjoy the mix of quilts and that you'll be putting your stash (or your newly purchased fabrics!) to beautiful use. We'd love to see what you create, so be sure to share your results at #TwoOfAKindQuilts.

---------------------- *- Happy scrap quilting -* ----------------------

Lissa & Susan

Meet our Machine Quilters

No matter how beautiful the fabrics and how precisely we sew our quilt tops, they just aren't complete until they've been quilted and bound. The quilting adds so much depth, texture, and even an occasional touch of whimsy. We each have a long-arm quilter we've worked with for years, and we want to introduce them to you. Our quilts just wouldn't be as lovely without their contributions.

MAGGI HONEYMAN

"Quilting can make or break the look of a quilt. Working with Maggi always complements my quilts, and her quilting adds that special touch without overpowering it. Maggi knows my style, makes great suggestions, and is willing to do some crazy stuff if I ask. (And I have.)" ~ Lissa

Maggi began quilting as a hobby about 30 years ago, and started machine quilting nine years later. Machine quilting as a job was a dive into the deep end after 20 years of doing in-home daycare. While Maggi hasn't studied art, she's always been a maker.

She had never tried long-arm quilting before heading to a quilt show to buy her first long-arm machine. Her first machine, a Gammill Classic with no stitch regulator, was not computerized and it's the machine she still quilts all her custom quilts with today. Years later, she added a Gammill Statler Stitcher (computerized and stitch-regulated) which she uses for all her edge-to-edge quilting. Maggi usually has both machines going at the same

"When I get a quilt back from Maggi, I hunt across the quilt top to find my name stitched somewhere in her quilting. It's such a fun touch. My quilts will be around long after I am gone. Having my name in the quilt is a piece of me that will carry on. I also have Maggi sign my quilt. Her work is just as big a part of the finished quilt as mine is." ~ Lissa

LISSA ALEXANDER WITH MAGGI HONEYMAN

time. In fact, there have been times when she's had both machines running from 7:30 a.m. to 11:30 p.m. for seven days in a row! It helps that she really loves what she does.

When Maggi bought her first long-arm, it took about a year of using it all day, every day before she felt proficient. Not trained in art or design, Maggi tells her customers, "I can quilt way better than I can draw," before showing them any quilting design sketches. After a year of machine quilting, she entered a quilt show with a hand-guided edge-to-edge design she'd done and won a blue ribbon. That gave her the confidence to keep on quilting and to build her business. While she hasn't kept track, she's pretty sure the number of quilts she's quilted is in the thousands.

Maggi says she's always felt grateful for return customers who want to use her services again. "That's a huge pat on the back to a machine quilter. I tell my customers 'thanks for quilting with me,' because I do feel like it is a collaboration between the two of us. It's heartwarming for me to get feedback from quiltmakers who see how I've quilted their quilt and share that they love what I did. It inspires me to do more!"

"Lissa has always been super generous with her praise for my work and appreciation for my input. I can always share what I envision for a quilt or ask if she's considered an option. She's effusive with admiration of the work that I do with her and that's heartwarming as a machine quilter." ~ Maggi

SUE ROGERS

"I know when I hand over a quilt top to Sue for her magic quilting, I won't be disappointed with the outcome. Sue is always a part of my sewing process so she is constantly thinking of a design that works well for the style of my quilts. She also has an eagle eye for spotting secondary patterns to play with for another design feature that I hadn't even noticed. I never hesitate working with Sue ... my only decision is which quilt from my stack that lives at her house is next in line." ~ Susan

Sue Rogers dreamed of working for a quilt shop. When she retired from a career in banking, that's exactly what she did. Much to her surprise, she was immediately assigned to the long-arm room. She had absolutely no experience in long-arm quilting, but she had to learn in a hurry. Back in the day, there was no stitch regulator or computer on the Gammil machine, but she quickly learned to do meander quilting—the type of quilting that was very common at the time.

Not only did Sue love running the quilting machine, but working in the shop was also where Sue and I met, as we were coworkers.

These days, Sue Rogers owns that very same quilting machine, although now it lives at her house. She's added a computer to it so she can quilt a huge array of pantograph patterns, or do custom quilting if she desires. Surprising no one, I'm her most prolific client. I make the quilt tops and, most of the time, Sue decides how to quilt them. Sometimes I have a preference, but we've worked together for so long that I trust Sue to quilt the perfect design every time.

As a bonus, Sue often asks me for some leftover or "orphan" blocks. (If you know me personally or through social media, you know I keep a bin of these blocks in my stash.) While I don't care for making pieced quilt backings, Sue loves to incorporate some of the leftovers into the quilt back for some extra spice. Talk about a great relationship! Don't we all need a Sue Rogers on speed dial?

SUSAN ACHE WITH SUE ROGERS

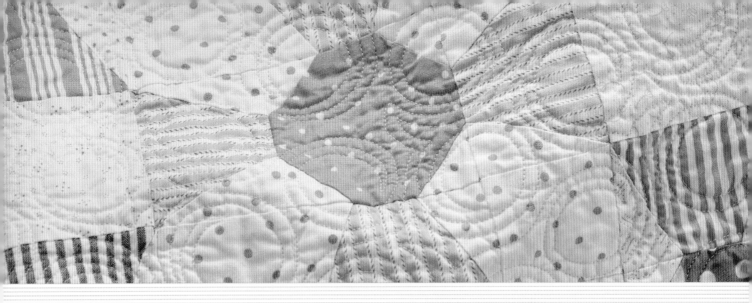

TWO OF A KIND

Daisy Squared

SUSAN ACHE

QUILT SIZE: 53½" × 73½" | BLOCK SIZE: 7" × 7"

What a fun block to make! I just pulled anything and everything out of my stash that was striped or polka-dotted and started playing. I buy these kinds of prints whenever I see them, but, even if you don't hoard them like I do, they won't be hard to find! Block construction isn't difficult; you're simply making the same block throughout the entire quilt. However, some blocks are only partially constructed to create the sashing.

MATERIALS

Yardage is based on 42"-wide fabric. Fat quarters are 18" × 21"; fat eighths are 9" × 21".

- 20 fat quarters of assorted light prints for blocks and sashing
- 20 fat eighths of assorted stripes for blocks and sashing
- 20 fat eighths of assorted dots for blocks and sashing
- 1½ yards of blue-and-white dot for sashing, border, and binding
- 3⅓ yards of fabric for backing
- 60" × 80" piece of batting
- Template plastic

CUTTING

All measurements include ¼" seam allowances. Trace triangle patterns A and B on page 19 onto template plastic and cut out on the drawn lines. Trace the templates onto the wrong side of the 3½"-wide strips as specified below, rotating the templates 180° after each cut to make the best use of your fabric.

From *each* of the 20 light print fat quarters, cut:
3 strips, 3½" × 21" (60 total); crosscut into:
- 12 *each* of triangle A and A reversed (240 total of each; 4 are extra)
- 3 squares, 3½" × 3½" (60 total; 2 are extra)

1 strip, 2½" × 21"; crosscut into 7 squares, 2½" × 2½" (160 total)
1 strip, 1½" × 21"; crosscut into 12 squares, 1½" × 1½" (240 total; 4 are extra)

From *each* of the 20 stripe fat eighths, cut:
2 strips, 3½" × 21" (40 total); crosscut into 12 of triangle B (240 total; 4 are extra)

From *each* of the 20 dot fat eighths, cut:
3 squares, 3½" × 3½" (60 total; 1 is extra)

From the blue-and-white dot, cut:
9 strips, 3½" × 42"; crosscut 2 of the strips into 20 pieces, 2½" × 3½"
7 strips, 2½" × 42"

MAKING THE BLOCKS

Press the seam allowances as indicated by the arrows.

1. To make one block, gather a set of matching light print pieces (four 2½" squares, four 1½" squares, and four each of triangle A and A reversed), four matching stripe B triangles, and one dot 3½" square.

2. Use a pencil to mark a diagonal line on the wrong side of each light 1½" square. Align a marked light square right side down on one corner of the dot 3½" square as shown. Sew on the drawn line. Trim the seam allowances to ¼" and press the resulting triangle toward the corner. Add three more marked squares in the same manner to make a snowball unit, which should measure 3½" square, including seam allowances.

Make 1 snowball unit, 3½" × 3½".

3. Sew together a light A triangle and a stripe B triangle. Add a matching A reversed triangle as shown to make a triangle unit. Make four triangle units, each 3½" square, including seam allowances.

Make 4 units, 3½" × 3½".

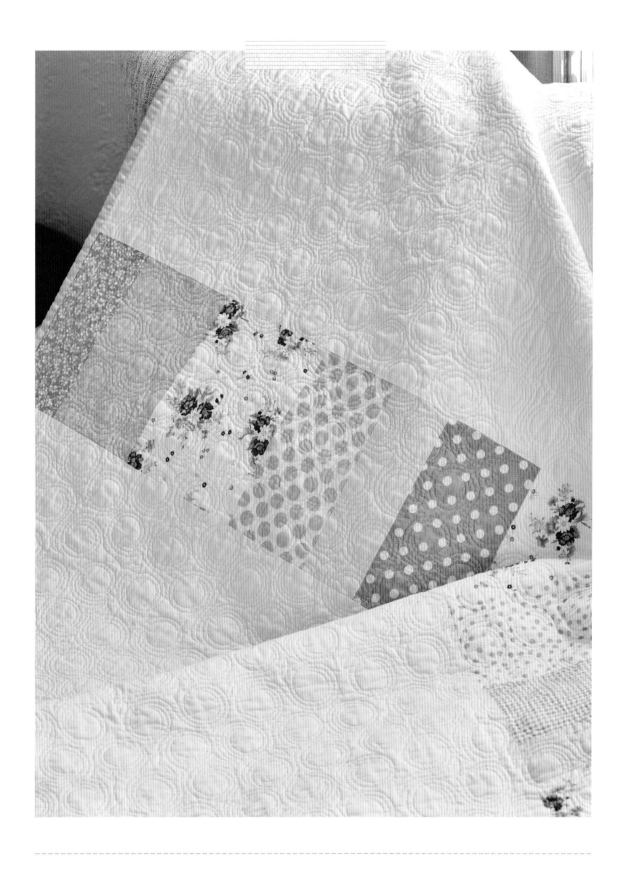

"I don't love making pieced backs, but I'm happy that my quilter does!" ~ Susan Ache

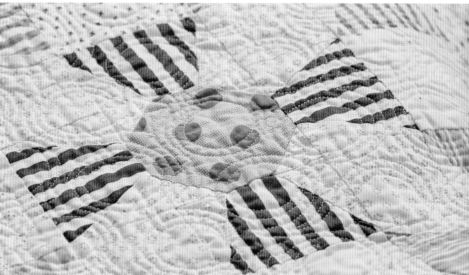

4. Trim 1" from the pointed tip of each triangle unit to make four side units, each 2½" × 3½", including seam allowances.

Make 4 units,
2½" × 3½".

5. Lay out the four light print 2½" squares, four side units, and one snowball unit in three rows. Sew together the pieces in rows. Join the rows to make a block measuring 7½" square, including seam allowances. Repeat to make 35 blocks total.

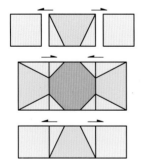
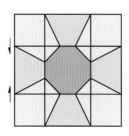

Make 35 blocks,
7½" × 7½".

6. To make a partial block for the sashing, gather a set of matching light print pieces (four 1½" squares and four each of triangle A and A reversed), four matching stripe B triangles, and one dot 3½" square. Repeat step 2 to make a snowball unit. Repeat steps 3 and 4 to make four side units. Do not sew the units together yet. Make 24 sets of sashing pieces total.

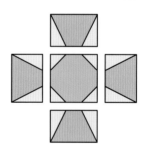

Make 24 sashing sets.

ASSEMBLING THE QUILT CENTER

1. Referring to the quilt assembly diagram on page 16, lay out the blocks in seven rows of five blocks each on a design wall or other large surface, leaving space between the blocks and rows to add sashing. At each intersection of four blocks, arrange the pieces from a sashing set. Between adjacent sashing sets, place a light print 3½" square. Place blue-and-white dot pieces at each end of the sashing rows.

Sue's Quilting Story

As soon as I saw this quilt, I knew I wanted to use some sort of a circular quilting motif to play off all the polka-dot fabrics. Not only does this design work well for the quilt top, it makes the back quite fun to look at too. (See photo on page 13.) For a bit of counterpoint to all the circles, I gleaned some scraps from Susan to use in the quilt backing, adding even more fun to the mix. I mean, why let those fun prints linger in a scrap basket when you can display them proudly on the back of your quilt? Each time you see them, it's a fun little surprise.

Sashing Placement

Don't be alarmed by the quilt assembly diagram below. Simply head to your design wall (or floor, or bed) and lay out your complete blocks, five per row, leaving space in between for sashing. Choose a sashing set and place the four parts so the top is in the first block row, the bottom is in the second block row, and the sides and center are in the sashing row. Think of it as placing the matching sashing pieces in the N, S, E, W positions, all pointing toward the snowball unit.

2. Sew together the three pieces in each short vertical sashing row. Then join the blocks and sashing pieces in each horizontal block row. Join the pieces in each long horizontal sashing row and press. Join all the rows to make a quilt center that is 47½" × 67½".

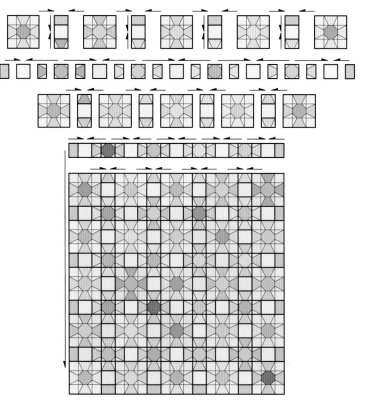

Quilt assembly

MAKING THE CUT

Strips and polka dots are such happy fabrics to me that I buy them whenever I'm building my stash. Sort through your stash—or add to it—for a good mix of both. I pulled out all my possible choices, then sorted them into *yes* and *no* piles. The fabrics on the right didn't make the cut. Too dark, diagonal stripes didn't work well with others, some dots were just too busy. Be like Goldilocks—be picky until you get just the right mix!

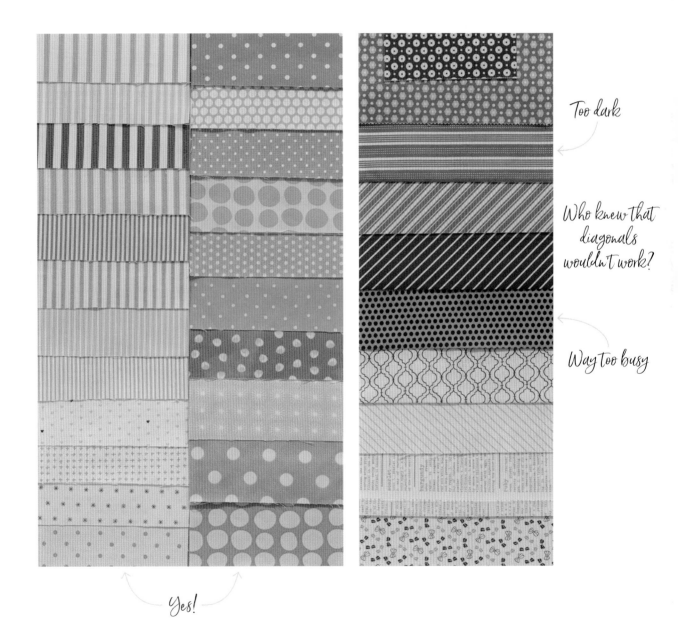

Too dark

Who knew that diagonals wouldn't work?

Way too busy

Yes!

ADDING THE BORDER

Join the blue-and-white dot 3½" × 42" strips end to end and press the seam allowances open. Trim the pieced length into two 67½"-long border strips and two 53½"-long border strips. Sew the 67½"-long strips to the sides of the center. Add the 53½"-long strips to the top and bottom to complete the quilt top, which should be 53½" × 73½".

FINISHING THE QUILT

For more details on any of the finishing steps, go to ShopMartingale.com/HowtoQuilt to download free illustrated information.

1. Prepare the quilt backing so that it is about 6" larger than the quilt top in both directions.

2. Layer the backing, batting, and quilt top; baste the layers together.

3. Quilt by hand or machine. Susan's quilt is machine quilted with an allover spiral design.

4. Using the blue-and-white dot 2½"-wide strips, make the binding and attach it to the quilt.

Quilt assembly

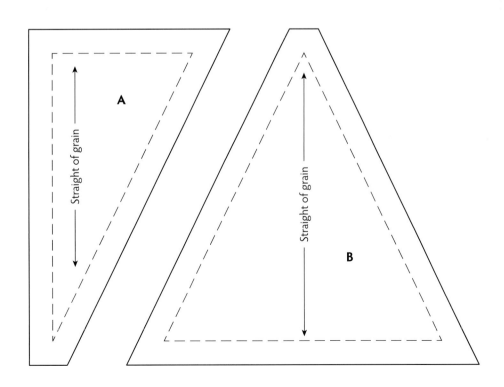

TWO OF A KIND

One by Two

LISSA ALEXANDER

QUILT SIZE: 72½" × 80½" | **BLOCK SIZE: 8" × 8"**

Are you a fan of leftovers? I am! I enjoy both the kind you find in the refrigerator and the kind I keep in my sewing room. If you like Jelly Rolls and Honey Buns, this is a perfect quilt to use up your leftover strips from other projects. This quick-to-stitch pattern makes a great gift for a college graduate, a special guy or gal in your life, or you could make two baby quilts at the same time.

Designed and pieced by **LISSA ALEXANDER**; quilted by **MAGGI HONEYMAN**

MATERIALS

Yardage is based on 42"-wide fabric. A Moda Jelly Roll contains 40 strips, 2½" × width of fabric. A Moda Honey Bun contains 40 strips, 1½" × width of fabric. Strip numbers given are estimates; your exact yardage will be determined by the different-width strips and whites or mediums you incorporate into your strip sets.

- 26 to 35 strips, 2½" × 42", of assorted medium prints in gray, yellow, green, pink, and coral for blocks
- 40 to 45 strips, 1½" × 42", of assorted medium prints in gray, yellow, green, pink, and coral for blocks
- 26 to 35 strips, 2½" × 42", of assorted white prints for blocks
- 40 to 45 strips, 1½" × 42", of assorted white prints for blocks
- ⅝ yard of multicolored print for binding
- 5 yards of fabric for backing
- 81" × 89" piece of batting

CUTTING

Measurements include ¼" seam allowances.

From the multicolored print, cut:
8 strips, 2½" × 42"

MAKING THE BLOCKS

Press all seam allowances toward the darker print.

1. Sew together enough 1½"-wide and 2½"-wide strips to make a strip set that measures 8½" × 42", including seam allowances. Use any of the strip-width arrangements shown. Lissa usually alternated between white and medium print strips, but you can vary that for interest. Make 23 strip sets.

Make 23 strip sets, 8½" × 42".

2. Crosscut each strip set into four segments, 8½" square, to make 92 blocks (2 are extra).

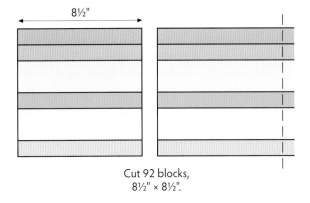

8½"

Cut 92 blocks,
8½" × 8½".

ASSEMBLING THE QUILT TOP

Press all seam allowances as indicated by the arrows.

1. Referring to the quilt assembly diagram below, lay out the blocks in 10 rows of nine blocks each. Starting at the upper-left block, Lissa arranged the first two adjacent blocks with seams running vertically, then two blocks with seams running horizontally, and so on. She alternated the next row to run perpendicular to the first row. She adjusted this layout at times for interest or to make sure seams abutted.

2. Sew together the blocks in each row. Join the rows to complete the quilt top, which should be 72½" × 80½".

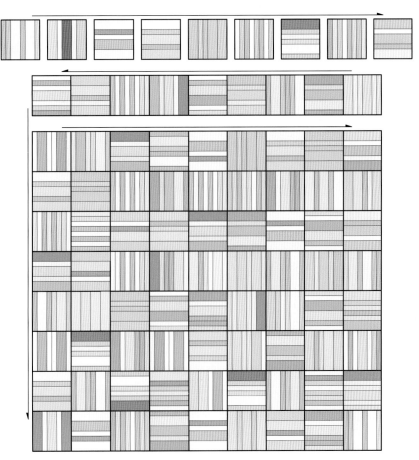

Quilt assembly

Maggi's Quilting Notes

Choosing an allover Baptist Fan quilting design was a way to add soft curves to a very linear, strippy quilt design. Lissa had done most of the hand embroidery on her top before it was quilted. Some quilters might be worried about stitching over the embroidery, but I wasn't. Up close, you'd notice that some of the handwork has been stitched over by the quilting. But once you step away to look at the overall design (which I think is how most people look at a quilt), it really doesn't detract from anything. Embroidering the top prior to quilting meant not worrying about burying the floss thread tails later. That's an extra win in my book!

Saving for a Rainy Day

As I square up fabric, I cut 1½"-wide strips to add to my stash of Honey Bun strips. I also cut leftovers from projects into 2½"-wide strips to add to my leftover Jelly Roll strips. I generally don't have an immediate plan, but rather save them until I have enough or the mood strikes me to pull them out and play with them to end up with a quilt like One by Two.

In addition, you can save the leftover cuts from the strip sets and incorporate them into the binding if desired.

FINISHING THE QUILT

For more details on any of the finishing steps, go to ShopMartingale.com/HowtoQuilt to download free illustrated information.

1. Prepare the quilt backing so that it is about 8" larger than the quilt top in both directions.

2. Layer the backing, batting, and quilt top; baste the layers together.

3. Quilt by hand or machine. Lissa's quilt is machine quilted with an allover Baptist fan pattern.

4. Using the multicolored print 2½"-wide strips, make the binding and attach it to the quilt.

MAKING THE CUT

When it comes to using Moda's precut Jelly Rolls and Honey Buns, I prefer to mix and match the strips rather than stick with just one collection. After deciding on my color scheme, I rummaged through my bins of leftover strips and decent sized scraps to look for all the soft greens, peaches, yellows, and similarly colored low-volume pieces. Most of these made the final cut, but you won't spy that green watering can print in the quilt. It was just too dark and dominant. Don't be afraid to edit your initial choices to get to a mix that's just right.

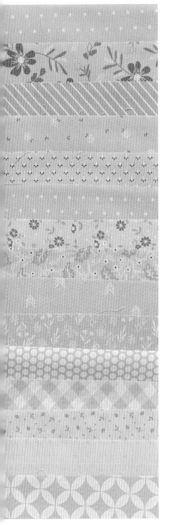

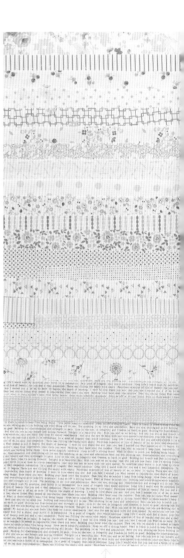

Too dark and busy

I love all these orange, green, and yellow low-volume prints!

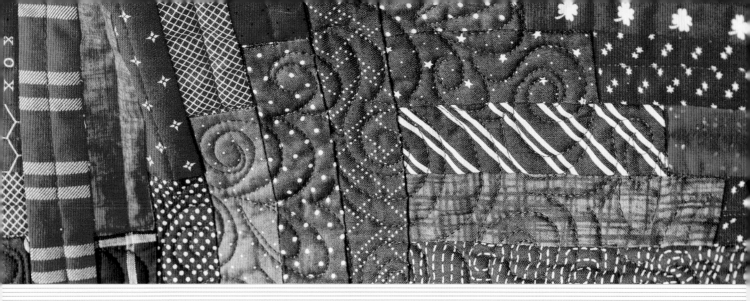

American Pavement

LISSA ALEXANDER

QUILT SIZE: 72½" × 72½" | **BLOCK SIZE: 6" × 6"**

Scrappy reds and blues pave the way for a Log Cabin look-alike with a twist. Patterned after brick pavers, the strip-pieced blocks come together to form rectangles rather than squares. Are the reds all the same shade? Not a chance. Are the blues all the same hue? Not if I can help it. When I'm making a two-color scrappy quilt, I'm hoping to use the most diverse mix of fabrics possible. Plaids, dots, checks, and prints all made the cut. Afraid to mix straight stripes and diagonal stripes? Don't be! Scrap quilting is like making a great vegetable soup. Throw in all you've got and watch the magic meld of flavors happen.

MATERIALS

Yardage is based on 42"-wide fabric.

- 60 squares, 10" × 10", of assorted blue prints for blocks
- 60 squares, 10" × 10", of assorted red prints for blocks
- ⅝ yard of dark blue print for binding
- 4½ yards of fabric for backing
- 81" × 81" piece of batting

CUTTING

All measurements include ¼" seam allowances.

From *each* of 24 blue print 10" squares, cut:
1 strip, 5½" × 10" (24 total)
1 strip, 3½" × 10" (24 total)

From *each* of 24 blue print 10" squares, cut:
1 strip, 4½" × 10" (24 total)
1 strip, 2½" × 10" (24 total)
1 strip, 1½" × 10" (24 total)

From *each* of the remaining 12 blue print 10" squares, cut:
6 strips, 1½" × 6½" (72 total)

From *each* of 24 red print 10" squares, cut:
1 strip, 5½" × 10" (24 total)
1 strip, 3½" × 10" (24 total)

From *each* of 24 red print 10" squares, cut:
1 strip, 4½" × 10" (24 total)
1 strip, 2½" × 10" (24 total)
1 strip, 1½" × 10" (24 total)

From *each* of the remaining 12 red print 10" squares, cut:
6 strips, 1½" × 6½" (72 total)

From the dark blue print, cut:
8 strips, 2½" × 42"

MAKING THE BLOCKS

Press the seam allowances in the directions indicated by the arrows.

1. Join a blue 1½" × 10" strip and a red 5½" × 10" strip to make strip set A measuring 6½" × 10". Make 24 of strip set A. Crosscut each strip set into six A segments, 1½" × 6½" (144 total).

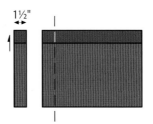

Make 24 A strip sets, 6½" × 10".
Cut 144 A segments, 1½" × 6½".

2. Join a blue 2½" × 10" strip and a red 4½" × 10" strip to make strip set B measuring 6½" × 10". Make 24 of strip set B. Crosscut each strip set into six B segments, 1½" × 6½" (144 total).

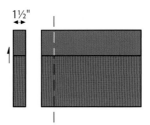

Make 24 B strip sets, 6½" × 10".
Cut 144 B segments, 1½" × 6½".

3. Join a blue 3½" × 10" strip and a red 3½" × 10" strip to make strip set C measuring 6½" × 10". Make 24 of strip set C. Crosscut each strip set into six C segments, 1½" × 6½" (144 total).

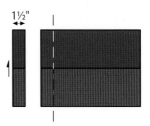

Make 24 C strip sets, 6½" × 10".
Cut 144 C segments, 1½" × 6½".

It's a mutual admiration society. When we see each other's quilts, we can't imagine not wanting to make that same quilt in that same color palette. Do you have a sewing buddy like that? Even though we don't compare our quilts in the construction phase, they're spot on when we show them to one another.

4. Join a blue 4½" × 10" strip and a red 2½" × 10" strip to make strip set D measuring 6½" × 10". Make 24 of strip set D. Crosscut each strip set into six D segments, 1½" × 6½" (144 total).

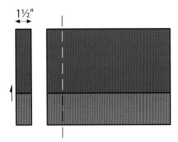

1½"

Make 24 D strip sets, 6½" × 10".
Cut 144 D segments, 1½" × 6½".

5. Join a blue 5½" × 10" strip and a red 1½" × 10" strip to make strip set E measuring 6½" × 10". Make 24 of strip set E. Crosscut each strip set into six E segments, 1½" × 6½" (144 total).

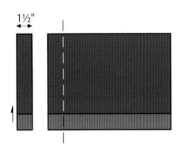

1½"

Make 24 E strip sets, 6½" × 10".
Cut 144 E segments, 1½" × 6½".

6. Join one each of segments A–E as shown to make a block unit measuring 5½" × 6½". Make 144 block units.

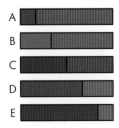
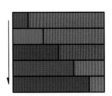

Make 144 units,
5½" × 6½".

7. Sew a red 1½" × 6½" strip to the top edge of a block unit as shown to make block A. Make 72 A blocks, each 6½" square, including seam allowances.

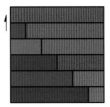

Make 72 A blocks,
6½" × 6½".

8. Sew a blue 1½" × 6½" strip to the bottom edge of a block unit as shown to make block B. Make 72 B blocks, each 6½" square, including seam allowances.

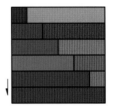

Make 72 B blocks,
6½" × 6½".

Oops!

Do as I say, not as I did. I inadvertently made some of my A and B blocks reversed from how I wanted them, but didn't notice until my quilt was quilted. Be sure to follow the block assembly diagrams closely! But don't worry if you goof like I did. It's not easy to spot the difference in the finished quilt.

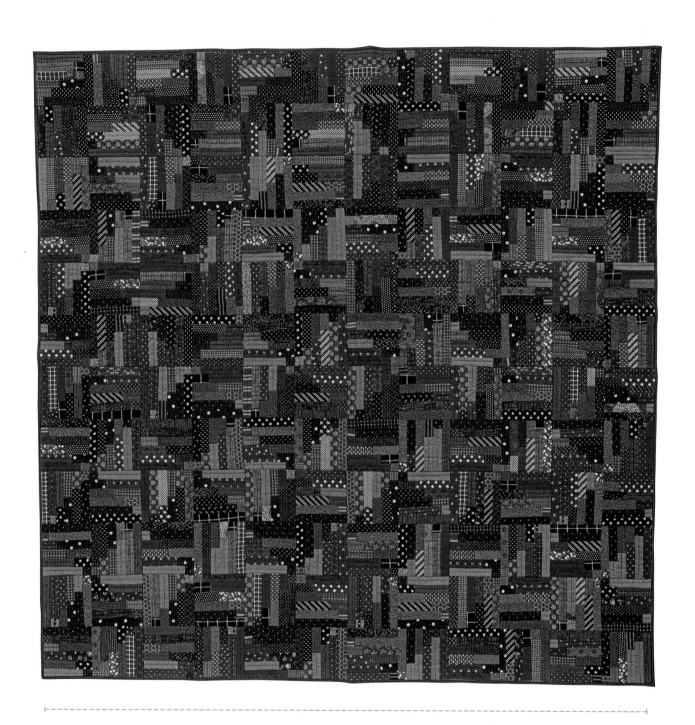

Designed and pieced by LISSA ALEXANDER; quilted by MAGGI HONEYMAN

Maggi's Quilting Notes

The twist of these blocks forming rectangles rather than squares made quilting this top a bit more challenging. I knew I wanted to treat the red and blue sections differently, but a circular design wouldn't work in the rectangles (like it might have if the blocks were squares). I tested some options by doodling designs on Press n' Seal see-through wrap. Ultimately I went with straight-line quilting in all the red spaces, both in the ditch and through the center of each piece. In the blue sections, I used a swirl design that I could adapt to fit the rectangular space. I also did something I rarely do. I changed thread colors to match the fabrics. This was a quilt where it felt right to keep contrast to a minimum.

ASSEMBLING THE QUILT TOP

Lay out the blocks in 12 rows of 12 blocks each, alternating blocks A and B and rotating them as shown in the quilt assembly diagram. Sew together the blocks in each row. Join the rows to complete the quilt top, which should be 72½" square.

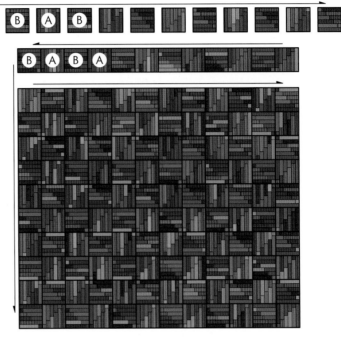

Quilt assembly

FINISHING THE QUILT

Go to ShopMartingale.com/HowtoQuilt to download free illustrated information if you need more details on any of the finishing steps.

1. Prepare the quilt backing so that it is about 8" larger than the quilt top in both directions.

2. Layer the backing, batting, and quilt top; baste the layers together.

3. Quilt by hand or machine. Lissa's quilt is machine quilted with straight lines through the center of each red strip and a swirl meander in the blue print areas.

4. Using the dark blue 2½"-wide strips, make the binding and attach it to the quilt.

"To make this quilt twice as nice, I sewed an improvised American flag for the back using larger cuts of fabric from my stash!" ~ Lissa

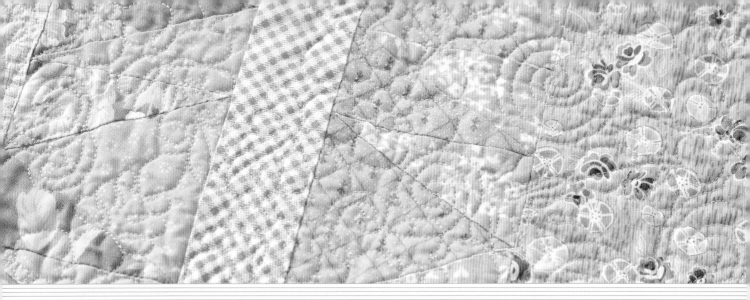

Ruffled Hibiscus

SUSAN ACHE

QUILT SIZE: 66½" × 66½" | BLOCK SIZE: 15" × 15"

If I have a favorite flowering plant, it's the coral hibiscus, more specifically the ruffled coral hibiscus. I am right on the edge of the climate that this plant loves, and because my house faces east and stays hot most of the time, this plant thrives in my front yard. This is a fun quilt to build because a coral hibiscus features many shades of the same color, and bold prints cut up very prettily in these blocks to mirror how colorful the flower actually is. If you have a big floral print you were waiting to use for a border, stop waiting and use it now in your blocks! You don't need tons of it. I loved making the individual parts of this quilt and then couldn't wait to see them all come together.

MATERIALS

Yardage is based on 42"-wide fabric. Fat quarters are 18" × 21"; fat eighths are 9" × 21".

- ⅝ yard of pink print for blocks
- 1 yard of coral print for blocks, sashing, and inner border
- 9 fat quarters of assorted green prints for blocks and inner-border corner units
- 12 squares, 10" × 10", of assorted green prints for inner border
- 9 fat eighths of assorted coral florals for blocks
- 12 squares, 10" × 10", of assorted coral florals for inner border
- ¾ yard of light coral gingham for sashing and inner border
- 1⅝ yards of multicolored floral for outer border and binding
- 4⅛ yards of fabric for backing
- 73" × 73" piece of batting
- Template plastic

CUTTING

All measurements include ¼" seam allowances. Trace patterns A and B on page 45 onto template plastic and cut out on the drawn lines. Trace the templates onto the wrong side of the 3½"-wide strips as specified below, rotating the templates 180° after each cut to make the best use of your fabric.

From the pink print, cut:

6 strips, 2" × 42"; crosscut into 36 strips, 2" × 6½"
5 strips, 1½" × 42"; crosscut into:
- 36 pieces, 1½" × 2½"
- 72 squares, 1½" × 1½"

From the coral print, cut:

5 strips, 3½" × 42"; crosscut into 64 of piece B
3 strips, 2" × 42"; crosscut into 52 squares, 2" × 2"
6 strips, 1½" × 42"; crosscut into 144 squares,
    1½" × 1½"

From *each* green print fat quarter, cut:

2 strips, 3½" × 21" (18 total); crosscut into 16 *each* of triangle A and A reversed (144 total A and 144 total A reversed)
1 strip, 1½" × 21" (9 total); crosscut into 4 pieces, 1½" × 2½" (36 total)

From scraps of green prints, cut *a total of:*

4 *each* of triangle A and A reversed (4 sets of matching A and A reversed pieces)

From *each* green print 10" square, cut:

2 strips, 3½" × 10" (24 total); crosscut into 5 *each* of triangle A and A reversed (60 total A and 60 total A reversed)

From *each* coral floral fat eighth, cut:

2 strips, 3½" × 21" (18 total); crosscut into:
- 12 *each* of triangle A and A reversed (108 total A and 108 total A reversed)
- 1 square, 2½" × 2½" (9 total)

From *each* coral floral 10" square, cut:

1 strip, 3½" × 10" (12 total); crosscut into 3 *each* of triangle A and A reversed (36 total A and 36 total A reversed)

From the light coral gingham, cut:

12 strips, 2" × 42"; crosscut into:
- 24 strips, 2" × 15½"
- 16 pieces, 2" × 3½"

From the multicolored floral, cut:

7 strips, 5" × 42"
7 strips, 2½" × 42"

MAKING THE BLOCK UNITS

Press the seam allowances as indicated by the arrows.

1. Sew together two pink 1½" squares and two coral print 1½" squares in pairs as shown. Join the pairs to make a four-patch unit that measures 2½" square, including seam allowances. Make 36 four-patch units.

Make 36 units,
2½" × 2½".

2. Use a pencil to mark a diagonal line on the wrong side of each remaining coral print 1½" square.

3. Align a marked square, right side down, on one end of a pink 1½" × 2½" piece as shown. Sew on the drawn line. Trim the seam allowances to ¼". Position and sew a second marked square on the opposite end of the pink piece to make a flying-geese unit that measures 1½" × 2½", including seam allowances. Make 36 flying-geese units.

Make 36 units,
1½" × 2½".

MAKING THE BLOCKS

Gather all of the pieces cut from one green print fat quarter and one coral floral fat eighth and use them in the following steps to make a block. Repeat the steps to make nine blocks.

1. Join a flying-geese unit and a green 1½" × 2½" piece to make a side unit that measures 2½" square, including seam allowances. Make four matching units.

Make 4 units,
2½" × 2½".

2. Lay out four of the four-patch units, four side units, and the coral floral 2½" square in three rows. Sew together the pieces in each row. Join the rows to make a unit that measures 6½" square, including seam allowances.

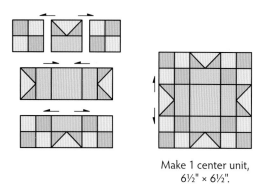

Make 1 center unit,
6½" × 6½".

3. Lay out four coral print 2" squares, four pink 2" × 6½" strips, and the unit from step 2 in three rows. Sew together the pieces in each row. Join the rows to make a center unit that measures 9½" square, including seam allowances.

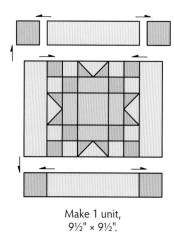

Make 1 unit,
9½" × 9½".

4. Sew a green A triangle to one edge of a coral B piece. Add a green A reversed triangle to the adjacent edge of the B piece as shown. Make four matching corner units, each 3½" square, including seam allowances.

Make 4 matching units,
3½" × 3½".

5. Sew together a green A reversed triangle and a coral floral A reversed triangle to make a unit that measures 2" × 3½", including seam allowances. Make 12 units. Using A triangles instead of reversed triangles, make 12 additional units.

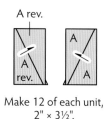

Make 12 of each unit,
2" × 3½".

6. Sew together three of each unit made in step 5 to make a rectangle unit that measures 3½" × 9½", including seam allowances. Make four matching units.

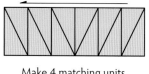

Make 4 matching units,
3½" × 9½".

7. Lay out four corner units from step 4, four rectangle units from step 6, and the center unit from step 3 in three rows as shown. Sew together the units in each row. Join the rows to make a block that measures 15½" square, including seam allowances. Repeat steps 1–7 to make nine blocks.

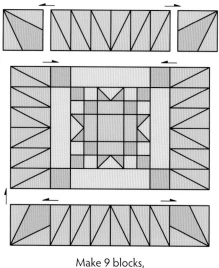

Make 9 blocks,
15½" × 15½".

MAKING THE CUT

Start by pulling out all the scraps that you think will work—anything that's in your desired color palette. Then don't be afraid to edit out whatever you don't think works so well. I wanted a variety of greens, but more or less in a mossy medium value. Same for the peaches—I wanted a lot of fabrics in assorted values, but nothing too dark or too busy.

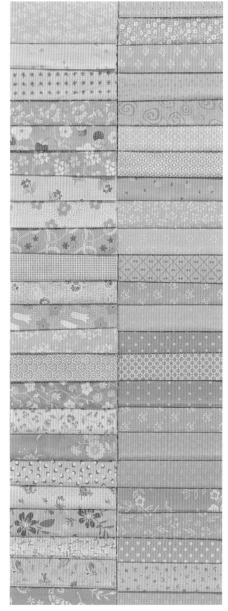

I love the color and scale of this print, but it reads like lavender.

Print scale too big

This dark one would grab all the attention.

Notice how all the greens work together, even though some are more yellow green and some are grayer.

ASSEMBLING THE QUILT CENTER

Referring to the quilt assembly diagram below, lay out the blocks, the 16 remaining coral print 2" squares, and the light coral gingham 2" × 15½" sashing strips in seven rows. Sew together the pieces in each row. Join the rows to make the quilt center, which should measure 51½" square, including seam allowances.

MAKING THE INNER-BORDER UNITS

Gather all of the pieces cut from one green print 10" square and one coral floral 10" square and use them in the following steps to make a border unit. Repeat the steps to make 12 inner-border units.

1. Referring to step 4 of "Making the Blocks" on page 40, make two matching corner units.

2. Referring to step 5 of "Making the Blocks," make three units each using A triangles and A reversed triangles.

3. Sew together the two corner units and the A and A reversed units to make a border unit that measures 3½" × 15½", including seam allowances. Repeat steps 1–3 to make 12 inner-border units.

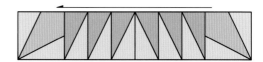

Make 12 inner-border units, 3½" × 15½".

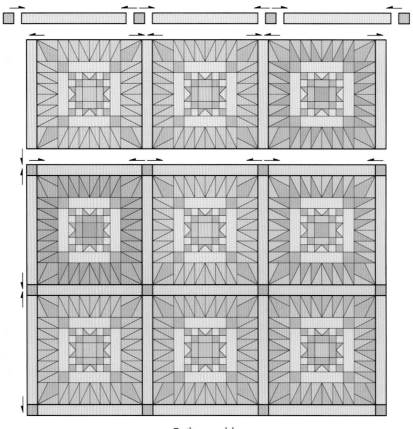

Quilt assembly

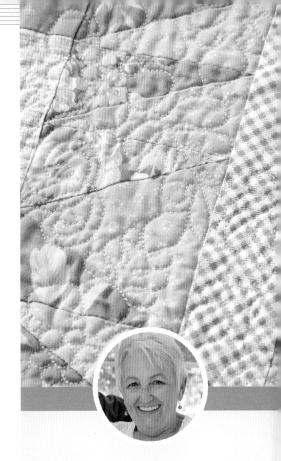

Use Templates to Create Drama

Many quilters act like *template* is a bad word. I'm here to tell you that I LOVE using templates to create interesting and dramatic shapes in quilt blocks. That kite shape in the corner units thrills me. So try your hand at making and using templates. Or cheat, like I do, and use the 3" Block-Loc Kite ruler set instead! It takes a little more fabric, but the results are worth it.

ASSEMBLING AND ADDING THE BORDERS

1. Referring again to step 4 of "Making the Blocks," make four corner units from the remaining green print A and A reversed triangles and remaining coral print B pieces.

2. Sew together four light coral gingham 2" × 3½" pieces and three inner-border units to make a border that measures 3½" × 51½", including seam allowances. Make two for the side inner borders.

Make 2 side inner borders,
3½" × 51½".

3. Sew together two corner units from step 1, four light coral gingham 2" × 3½" pieces, and three inner-border units to make a top border that measures 3½" × 57½", including seam allowances. Repeat to make a bottom inner border.

Make 2 top/bottom inner borders,
3½" × 57½".

4. Sew the side inner-border strips to the side edges of the quilt top. Add the top and bottom inner-border strips to the remaining edges. The quilt top should measure 57½" square, including seam allowances.

Sue's Quilting Story

This is one of those quilts that is so packed with the beautiful patchwork that just about any quilting design I could use wouldn't really show. And that's perfectly fine. The way I look at quilting is that it's the backup singer. The fabrics and the quilt pattern should be the stars of the show. To me, a quilt like this just doesn't warrant the time and expense of custom quilting. I used a favorite pantograph pattern that has the occasional flower motif since this is a hibiscus quilt. But really, in this case it was just about adding texture.

Designed and pieced by SUSAN ACHE; quilted by SUE ROGERS

5. Join the multicolored floral 5" × 42" strips end to end and press the seam allowances open. Trim the pieced strip into two 66½"-long strips for the top and bottom outer borders and two 57½"-long strips for the side outer borders. Sew the side outer-border strips to the sides of the quilt top. Add the top and bottom outer-border strips to the top and bottom to complete the quilt top, which should be 66½" square.

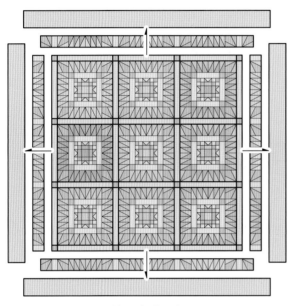

Adding the borders

FINISHING THE QUILT

For more details on any of the finishing steps, go to ShopMartingale.com/HowtoQuilt to download free illustrated information.

1. Prepare the quilt backing so that it is about 6" larger than the quilt top in both directions.

2. Layer the backing, batting, and quilt top; baste the layers together.

3. Quilt by hand or machine. Susan's quilt is machine quilted with an allover spiral-and-flower design.

4. Using the multicolored floral 2½"-wide strips, make the binding and attach it to the quilt.

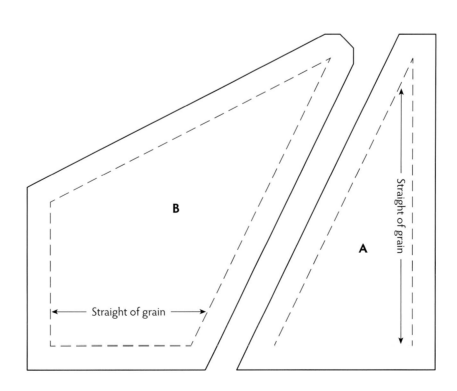

Windjammer

SUSAN ACHE

QUILT SIZE: 66½" × 66½" | BLOCK SIZE: 8" × 8"

I may not own a windjammer in real life, but I am certainly the master of my paper boat flotilla! Third-grade Vacation Bible School is when I learned to make paper-hat sailboats. I remember nothing about the circumstances, but I do remember going home to my family's pile of newspapers and making a complete fleet of sailboats with the black-and-white prints, the comics, and even the ads. Making the boats from fabric is simple; don't worry about the direction of your chosen fabric—when folding paper, it ends up being a mix of sideways, upside down, and right side up, and that's the same effect you want with your fabric.

MATERIALS

Yardage is based on 42"-wide fabric. Fat eighths are 9" × 21".

- 1 yard of white newspaper print for sailboats in blocks
- 12 fat eighths of assorted aqua prints for block backgrounds and inner border
- 13 strips, 2½" × 42", of assorted blue prints for Irish Chain blocks
- 13 fat eighths of assorted white prints for blocks and inner border (Susan used twice this number of fat eighths to make her quilt super scrappy.)
- ¾ yard of teal solid for blocks and inner border
- 1½ yards of blue floral for outer border and binding
- 4⅛ yards of fabric for backing
- 73" × 73" piece of batting
- Template plastic

Go for the Bold!

The bolder the background fabric, the more visible the paper boats become. So even if a fabric was the right color, I didn't use it if it had a directional or very busy print. Because the text print fabrics have so much going on, the busy background prints just seemed to fight with them for attention.

As for the text prints, try to mix them up within a block for different shading. It makes your boats look like they've really been made out of folded paper!

CUTTING

All measurements include ¼" seam allowances. Trace patterns A and B on page 57 onto template plastic and cut out on the drawn lines. Trace the templates onto the wrong side of the 4½"-wide strips as specified below, rotating the templates 180° after each cut to make the best use of your fabric.

From the white newspaper print, cut:
2 strips, 4½" × 21"; crosscut into 24 of triangle B
9 strips, 2½" × 42"; crosscut into:
- 48 pieces, 2½" × 4½"
- 48 squares, 2½" × 2½"

From *each* aqua print fat eighth, cut:
1 strip, 4½" × 21" (12 total); crosscut into:
- 4 pieces, 2½" × 4½" (48 total)
- 2 *each* of triangle A and A reversed (24 A total and 24 A reversed total)
4 squares, 2½" × 2½" (48 total)
4 strips, 1½" × 6½" (48 total)

From scraps of all aqua prints, cut *a total of*:
16 strips, 1½" × 6½"

From *each* blue print strip, cut:
8 pieces, 1½" × 4½" (104 total; 4 are extra)

From the assorted white prints, cut:
112 strips, 1½" × 6½"
100 pieces, 1½" × 2½"
128 squares, 1½" × 1½"

From the teal solid, cut:
2 strips, 2½" × 42"; crosscut into 25 squares, 2½" × 2½"
13 strips, 1½" × 42"; crosscut into 328 squares, 1½" × 1½"

From the blue floral, cut:
7 strips, 4½" × 42"
7 strips, 2½" × 42"

MAKING THE CUT

As a native Floridian, I cannot get enough of beautiful blue water and sandy beaches. So you can bet I have a lot of fabrics to fit that theme in my stash. While I thought some additional text prints and busier prints *(below right)* would work, they just detracted from the star of the show—the newsprint boat fabric. I didn't want to sink my plans, so I opted for calmer prints *(below left)* and smoother sailing for my flotilla.

Just right!

Busier prints didn't play nice with my main newsprint fabric

"Lissa and I always seem to lean toward our own sides of the
color wheel. After seeing her Sunshine Day (page 59),
I can't wait to play on her side of the wheel!" ~ Susan

MAKING THE SAILBOAT BLOCKS

Press the seam allowances as indicated by the arrows. Use one aqua print for each block in the steps that follow. Repeat the steps to make 24 blocks total.

1. Sew an aqua A triangle to one edge of a newspaper print B triangle; be sure the blunt tip of the B triangle is pointing up. Add a matching A reversed triangle to the adjacent edge of the B triangle as shown. The sail unit should measure 4½" square, including seam allowances.

Make 1 unit,
4½" × 4½".

2. Use a pencil to mark a diagonal line on the wrong side of two aqua 2½" squares and two newspaper print 2½" squares.

3. Align a marked aqua square, right side down, on one end of a newspaper print 2½" × 4½" piece as shown. Sew on the drawn line. Trim the seam allowances to ¼". Position and sew a marked newspaper print square on the opposite end of the newspaper print piece to make a flying-geese unit that measures 2½" × 4½", including seam allowances.

Make 1 unit,
2½" × 4½".

4. Using the same pieces but in reverse order, repeat step 3 to make a reversed flying-geese unit.

Make 1 reversed unit,
2½" × 4½".

5. Lay out four assorted white print 1½" squares, two aqua 1½" × 6½" strips, two aqua 2½" × 4½" pieces, the sail unit from step 1, and the flying-geese units from steps 3 and 4 in four rows as shown. Sew together the pieces in each row. Join the rows to make a Sailboat block that measures 8½" square, including seam allowances. Make 24 blocks.

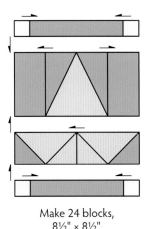

Make 24 blocks,
8½" × 8½".

MAKING THE CHAIN BLOCKS

To ensure that the same blue print surrounded each Sailboat block in the finished quilt, Susan placed all of her Sailboat blocks on a design wall and arranged the pieces for the Chain blocks around them before piecing any of the Chain blocks. (See the quilt assembly diagram on page 55.)

1. Lay out four teal solid 1½" squares, four assorted white print 1½" × 2½" pieces, and one teal solid 2½" square in three rows as shown. Sew together the pieces in each row. Join the rows to make a

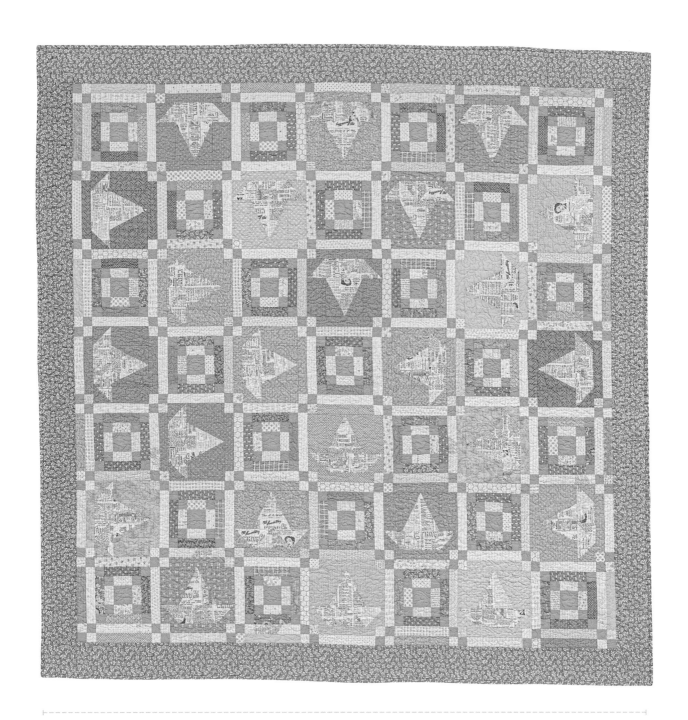

Designed and pieced by SUSAN ACHE; quilted by SUE ROGERS

center unit that measures 4½" square, including seam allowances. Make 25 center units.

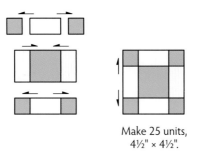

Make 25 units,
4½" × 4½".

2. Lay out four teal solid 1½" squares, four assorted blue print 1½" × 4½" pieces, and a center unit from step 1 in three rows as shown. Sew together the pieces in each row. Join the rows. The unit should now measure 6½" square, including seam allowances. Make 25.

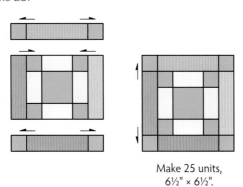

Make 25 units,
6½" × 6½".

3. Lay out four teal solid 1½" squares, four assorted white print 1½" × 6½" strips, and a center unit from step 2 in three rows as shown. Sew together the pieces in each row. Join the rows to make a Chain block that measures 8½" square, including seam allowances. Make 25 blocks.

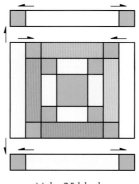

Make 25 blocks,
8½" × 8½".

ASSEMBLING THE QUILT CENTER

Referring to the quilt assembly diagram, lay out the blocks in seven rows of seven blocks each, alternating the Chain and Sailboat blocks and rotating the Sailboat blocks as shown. Sew together the blocks in each row. Join the rows to make the quilt center, which should measure 56½" square, including seam allowances.

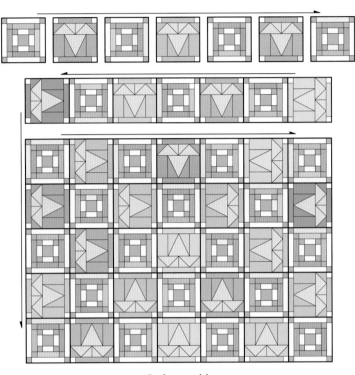

Quilt assembly

ASSEMBLING AND ADDING THE BORDERS

1. Referring to the diagram, sew together eight assorted white print 1½" squares, four assorted aqua 1½" × 6½" strips, six teal solid 1½" squares, and three assorted white print 1½" × 6½" strips to make a border that measures 1½" × 56½", including seam allowances. Make four.

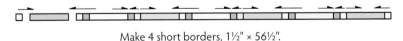

Make 4 short borders, 1½" × 56½".

2. Sew a teal solid 1½" square to each end of a border strip from step 1 to make a border that measures 1½" × 58½", including seam allowances. Make two for the top and bottom inner borders.

Make 2 top/bottom borders, 1½" × 58½".

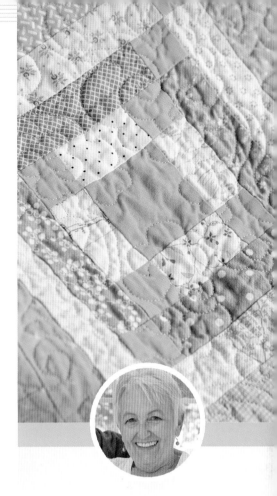

Sue's Quilting Story

Working with Susan Ache is so easy because she might have a nugget of an idea in mind, like "I'd like something watery," but she trusts me to come up with the goods. Riding the waves with this one, I chose a pantograph that not only featured waves, but also created the look of foam. Can't you just picture a little sailboat bobbing up and down on the waves? Every quilt tells a story, and the quilting designs need to to be a part of that story.

3. Sew the pieced border strips from step 1 to opposite edges of the quilt center. Add the pieced border strips from step 2 to the remaining edges.

4. Join the blue floral 4½" × 42" strips end to end and press the seam allowances open. Trim the pieced strip into two 58½"-long strips for the side outer borders and two 66½"-long strips for the top and bottom outer borders.

5. Sew the side outer-border strips to opposite edges of the quilt top. Add the top and bottom outer-border strips to the remaining edges to complete the quilt top, which should be 66½" square.

FINISHING THE QUILT

For more details on any of the finishing steps, go to ShopMartingale.com/HowtoQuilt to download free illustrated information.

1. Prepare the quilt backing so that it is about 6" larger in both directions than the quilt top.

2. Layer the backing, batting, and quilt top; baste the layers together.

3. Quilt by hand or machine. Susan's quilt is machine quilted with an allover design of ocean waves and spirals.

4. Using the blue floral 2½"-wide strips, make the binding and attach it to the quilt.

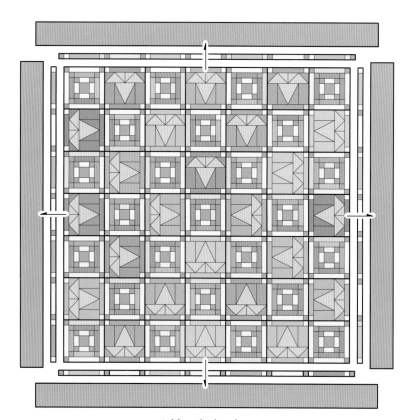

Adding the borders

"Two things that I'll never get tired of are making a plan for a quilt and repetitive sewing. I love to make blocks and I love to give myself a mental high five when I accomplish the little sewing goals I set for myself." ~ Susan

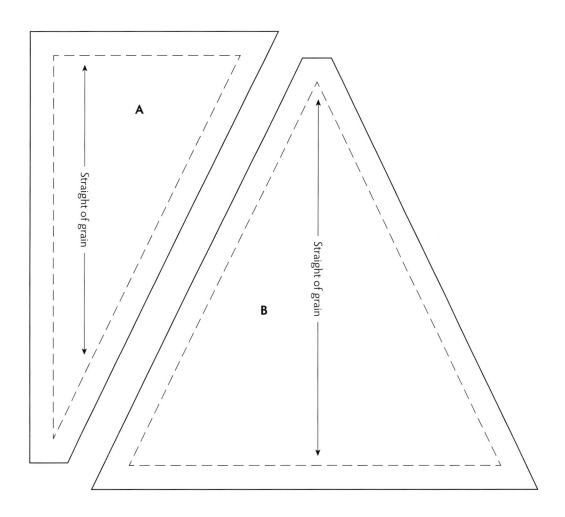

A

Straight of grain

B

Straight of grain

Sunshine Day

LISSA ALEXANDER

QUILT SIZE: 72½" × 72½" | **BLOCK SIZE: 18" × 18"**

"I think I'll go for a walk outside now. The summer sun's callin' my name. (I hear ya now.) I just can't stay inside all day. I've gotta get out, get me some of those rays . . ." That's what the Brady Bunch sang back in the '70s, and if I catch the first few bars, I can hum it all day as I play in my quilting room with a sunrise assortment of prints. When quilters can't see their way to mixing oranges, pinks, and yellows, I refer them to the summer sky and its brilliant mix of those hues. As the song says, "Can't you dig the sunshine? Can't you hear him callin' your name? The summer sun shows me the way!"

MATERIALS

Yardage is based on 42"-wide fabric. Fat quarters are 18" × 21"; fat eighths are 9" × 21".

- ⅓ yard *each* of 8 assorted light prints for block A and B backgrounds
- ⅓ yard *each* of 8 assorted light prints for block A and C backgrounds
- 32 fat eighths *OR* 11 fat quarters of assorted warm prints in yellow, orange, coral, pink, and red for blocks
- ⅝ yard of orange check for binding
- 4½ yards of fabric for backing
- 79" × 79" piece of batting
- Template plastic

CUTTING

All measurements include ¼" seam allowances. Trace patterns A–C on pages 67–69 onto template plastic and cut out on the drawn lines. Trace the A template onto the wrong side of the warm print 5"-wide strips as specified below, rotating the template 180° after each cut to make the best use of your fabric.

From *each of 8* of the light prints, cut:
4 of piece B (32 total)

From *each* of the remaining 8 light prints, cut:
4 of piece C (32 total)

From scraps of remaining light prints, cut *a total of:*
64 of triangle A

From the assorted warm prints, cut:
32 strips, 5" × 21"; crosscut *each* strip into 7 of triangle A (224 total)

From the orange check, cut:
8 strips, 2½" × 42"

MAKING THE BLOCKS

Instructions that follow are for chain piecing, but if you'd like to make one block at a time, lay out the pieces for each block before completing these steps. Use four kite units with the same matching light print, and pay attention to matching the marked dots shown in the diagrams when joining pieces. Press the seam allowances in the directions indicated by the arrows.

1. Matching the dots, sew a warm print A triangle to either side of a light print A triangle. Add a third warm print A triangle to the top edge to make a pieced triangle. Make 64 pieced triangles.

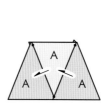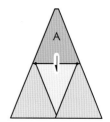

Make 64 pieced triangles.

2. Matching the dots, sew a warm print A triangle to a light print B piece to make a kite unit. Make 32 kite units.

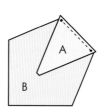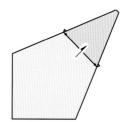

Make 32 kite units.

3. Sew together a pieced triangle and a kite unit to make a quarter block. Make 32 quarter blocks.

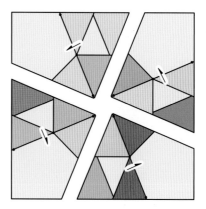

Make 32 quarter blocks.

Fussy Cutting to the Rescue

When cutting the pieces for this quilt, I generally followed the grainline indicated on the pattern pieces. However, there were times when I decided to throw caution to the wind and fussy-cut pieces to take advantage of the fabric design. For example, sometimes I'd cut the C pieces so a stripe would run diagonally in the finished block, rather than horizontally or vertically. I think it adds a bit of flair. Just be careful, as the outer edges of those pieces will be on the bias and a bit stretchier than the other block edges.

4. Join two quarter blocks to make a half block. Make 16 half blocks.

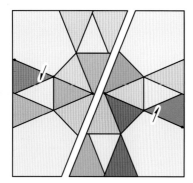

Make 16 half blocks.

5. Sew together two half blocks to make block A measuring 18½" square, including seam allowances. Make eight A blocks.

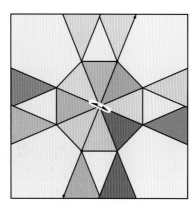

Make 8 A blocks,
18½" × 18½".

6. Using four matching light print C pieces instead of kite units, repeat steps 3–5 to make 32 quarter blocks, 16 half blocks, and then eight B blocks. Be sure to press as shown so that the seams will nest with the A blocks in the finished quilt.

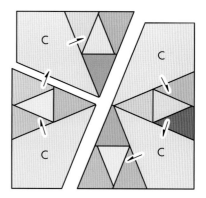

Make 8 B blocks,
18½" × 18½".

62 | TWO-OF-A-KIND QUILTS

"Two colors I'll never get enough of combining in quilts are pink and orange. It's like a fabulous combination of raspberry and orange sherbets, and the lights are the frosty parfait glasses that hold them." ~ Lissa

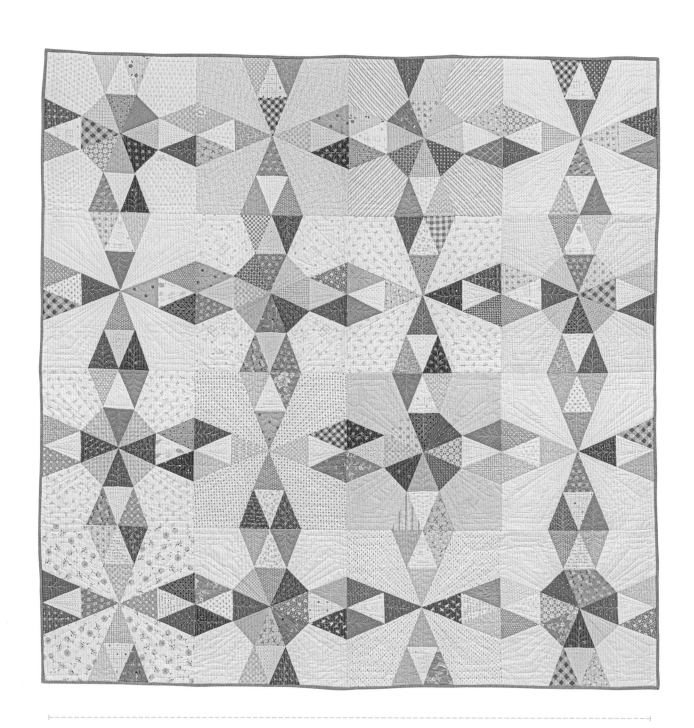

Designed and pieced by **LISSA ALEXANDER**; quilted by **MAGGI HONEYMAN**

ASSEMBLING THE QUILT TOP

Lay out the blocks in four rows of four blocks each, alternating blocks A and B as shown in the quilt assembly diagram. Sew together the blocks in each row. Join the rows to complete the quilt top, which should be 72½" square.

Quilt assembly

FINISHING THE QUILT

Go to ShopMartingale.com/HowtoQuilt to download free illustrated information if you need more detail on any of the finishing steps.

1. Prepare the quilt backing so that it is about 6" larger in both directions than the quilt top.

2. Layer the backing, batting, and quilt top; baste the layers together.

3. Quilt by hand or machine. Lissa's quilt is machine quilted with echoed kite shapes inside the B and C pieces. Most of the warm print A triangles are filled with a feathered leaf design, and the light print A triangles feature echoed triangle quilting.

4. Using the orange check 2½"-wide strips, make the binding and attach it to the quilt.

Maggi's Quilting Notes

When I saw this top I thought it was the perfect mix of modern colors and traditional blocks. Therefore, the goal for the quilting was to blend the two. I chose a mostly straight line design that echoes the diamond shapes in the four points of the light Friendship Stars formed where the block corners meet. To bring in a bit of a traditional look, I stitched feathers (is there a more classic quilting design?) in the pink and orange triangles. What I love about Lissa's mix of colors is the occasional butterscotch or salmon triangle in the mix. Nothing too matchy-matchy here!

MAKING THE CUT

I love corals and pinks mixed with yellow. What could be happier? As you can see,
I pulled out all the scraps (and all the stops!) when it came to some of my favorite fabrics.
Even small pieces worked their way into Sunshine Day. On top of that, I was going to
use creams for the backgrounds, but things started to look too dull and not so happy.
Instead, I opted for some low-volume scraps for the backgrounds to pump up the fun.

 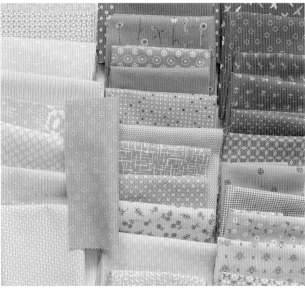

*My original plan
for background
didn't make it
to the final cut.*

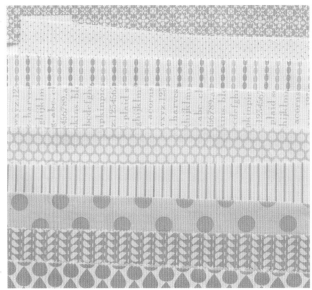

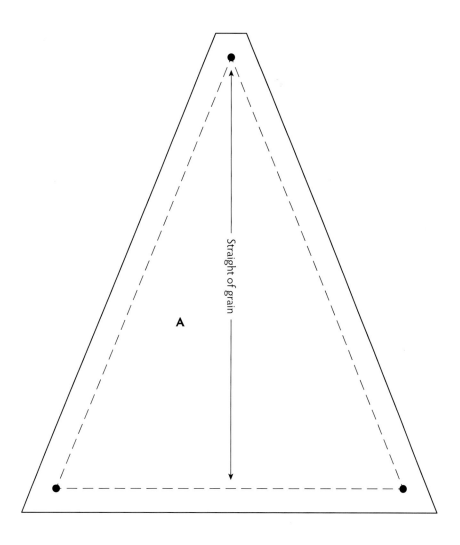

Straight of grain

A

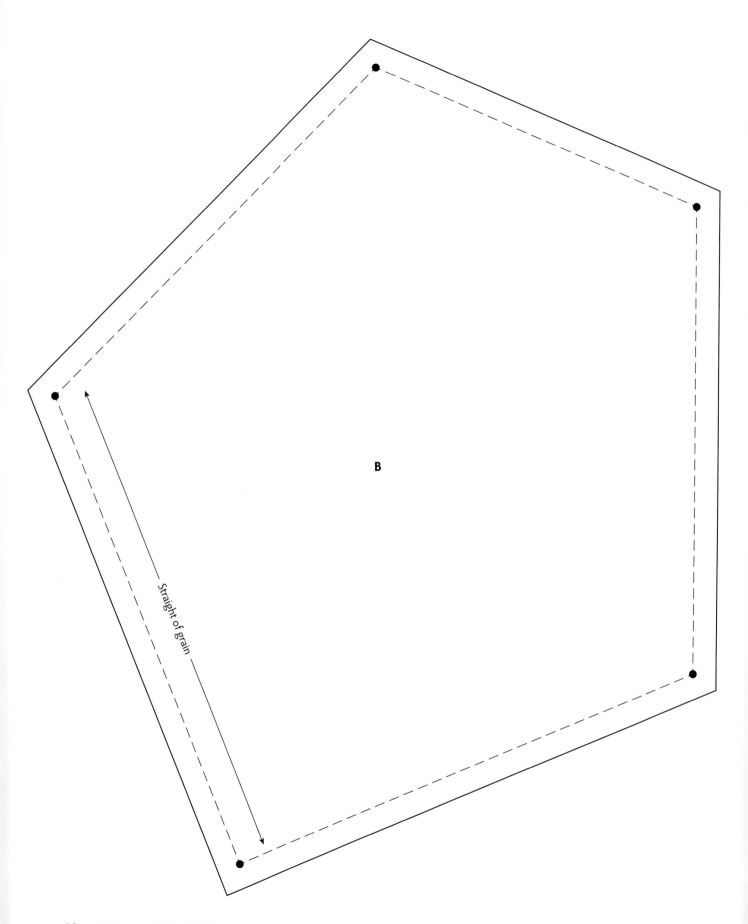

B

Straight of grain

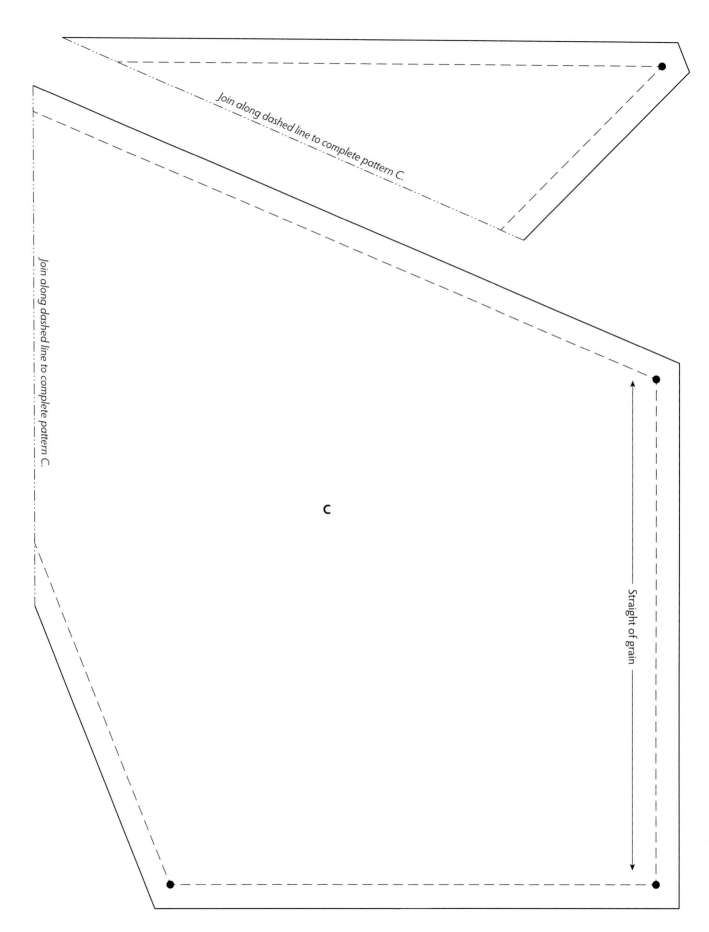

Join along dashed line to complete pattern C.

Join along dashed line to complete pattern C.

C

Straight of grain

SCRAPS GONE WILD

Big Wreaths

LISSA ALEXANDER

QUILT SIZE: 82½" × 82½" | **BLOCK SIZE:** 32" × 32"

One of my favorite ways to accumulate a variety of 2½"-square scraps is by collecting mini charm packs. Though I do enjoy seeing all the pieces of a collection together, I usually pull the packs apart and sort the squares by color in a divided container with a hinged lid (think about the kinds of boxes meant for storing embroidery thread, fishing tackle, or art supplies). Then when it comes time to make a super-scrappy quilt, I grab my box and start pulling squares. What fun! I thought about making six wreaths, but thinking about a bigger-than-king-size quilt, I stopped myself at four. My, oh my, I do love scraps!

"It's not a race. Quilting's all for fun. It's an enjoyable way to set little personal goals for yourself that you can knock out of the park." ~ Susan

MATERIALS

Yardage is based on 42"-wide fabric.

- 4 yards *total* of assorted medium and dark prints for blocks and sashing units
- 5¼ yards *total* of assorted light prints for blocks, sashing units, and binding
- 7⅝ yards of fabric for backing
- 91" × 91" piece of batting

CUTTING

All measurements include ¼" seam allowances.

From the assorted medium and dark prints, cut a *total* of:

773 squares, 2½" × 2½"

From the assorted light prints, cut a *total* of:

32 pieces, 4½" × 8½"

32 squares, 4½" × 4½"

Enough 2½"-wide strips in lengths ranging from
    6" to 42" to total 350" in length for binding

Enough 2½"-wide strips in lengths ranging from
    2½" to 18" to total 275" in length for outer
    sashing strips

24 strips, 2½" × 14½"

32 strips, 2½" × 12½"

36 squares, 2½" × 2½"

MAKING THE BLOCKS

Press the seam allowances in the directions indicated by the arrows.

1. Sew together four assorted medium and dark print 2½" squares in two rows as shown. Join the rows to make a four-patch unit that measures 4½" square, including seam allowances. Make 160 units.

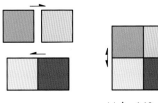

Make 160 units,
4½" × 4½".

2. Sew together four of the four-patch units in two rows as shown. Join the rows to make a 16-patch unit that measures 8½" square, including seam allowances. Make 32 units.

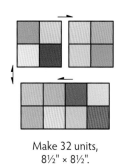

Make 32 units,
8½" × 8½".

3. Join a light 4½" square to the top edge of one four-patch unit. Add a light print 4½" × 8½" piece to the left edge to make a corner unit that measures 8½" square, including seam allowances. Make 32 units.

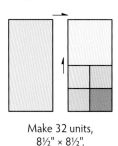

Make 32 units,
8½" × 8½".

4. Lay out two corner units and two 16-patch units, rotating the corner units as shown. Join the rows to make a quarter unit that measures 16½" square, including seam allowances. Make 16 quarter units.

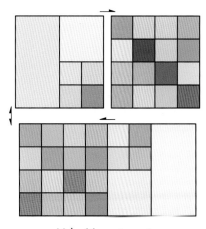

Make 16 quarter units,
16½" × 16½".

5. Lay out four quarter units in two rows, rotating the units as shown. Join the rows to make a block that measures 32½" square, including seam allowances. Make four blocks.

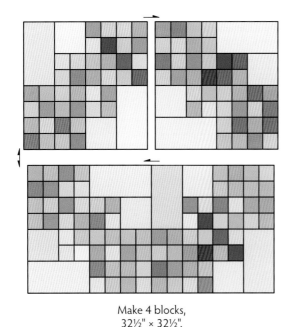

Make 4 blocks,
32½" × 32½".

MAKING THE SASHING UNITS

1. Sew together five assorted medium and dark print 2½" squares and four assorted light print 2½" squares in three rows as shown. Join the rows to make a nine-patch unit that measures 6½" square, including seam allowances. Make nine units.

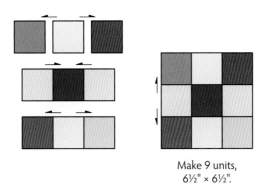

Make 9 units,
6½" × 6½".

2. Sew together the assorted light print 2½"-wide strips for the sashing and press the seam allowances open. Trim the pieced strip into eight strips, 32½" long.

3. Arrange one pieced strip from step 2, two light print 2½" × 14½" strips, six medium and dark print squares, and two light print 2½" × 12½" strips in three rows as shown. Sew the pieces together into rows. Join the rows to make an outer sashing unit that measures 6½" × 32½", including seam allowances. Make eight outer sashing units.

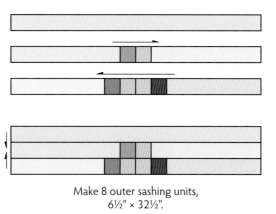

Make 8 outer sashing units,
6½" × 32½".

4. Arrange four light print 2½" × 12½" strips, 10 medium and dark print squares, and two light print 2½" × 14½" strips in three rows. Sew the pieces together into rows. Join the rows to make an inner sashing unit that measures 6½" × 32½", including seam allowances. Make four inner sashing units.

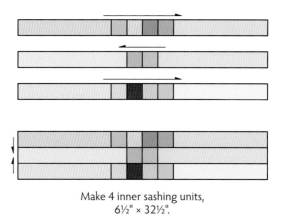

Make 4 inner sashing units,
6½" × 32½".

ASSEMBLING THE QUILT TOP

Referring to the quilt assembly diagram on page 77, lay out the nine-patch units, outer sashing units, blocks, and inner sashing units in five rows. Sew

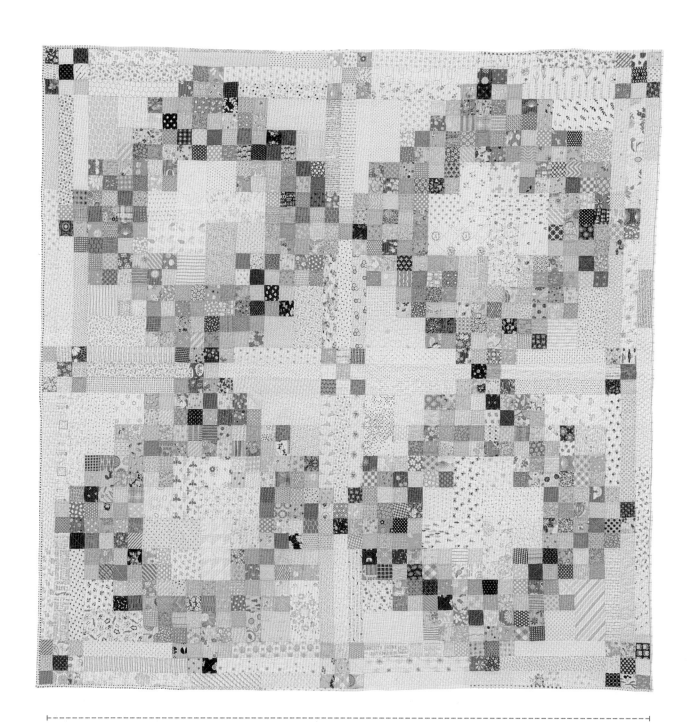

Designed and pieced by LISSA ALEXANDER; quilted by MAGGI HONEYMAN

together the pieces in each row. Join the rows to complete the quilt top, which should be 82½" square.

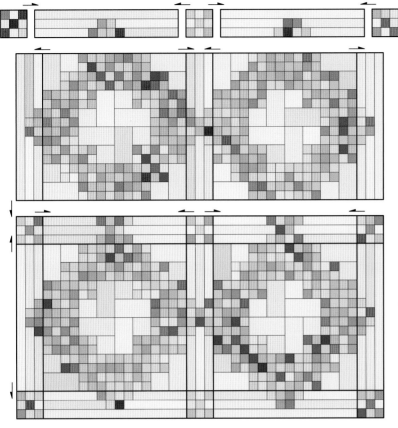

Quilt assembly

FINISHING THE QUILT

Go to ShopMartingale.com/HowtoQuilt to download free illustrated information if you need more details about any of the finishing steps.

1. Prepare the quilt backing so that it is about 8" larger in both directions than the quilt top.

2. Layer the backing, batting, and quilt top; baste the layers together.

3. Quilt by hand or machine. Lissa's quilt is machine quilted in the light print areas with a variety of designs, including ribbon candy, straight parallel lines, feathered leaves, and spirals. The medium and dark print squares are each quilted diagonally through the center and with curved lines connecting from seam to seam.

4. Using the assorted light print 2½"-wide strips, make the binding and attach it to the quilt.

Maggi's Quilting Notes

Accentuating the big wreaths was job number one, and I think the orange-peel design on the scrappy squares of each wreath draws attention to them. But it left lots of negative space in the light areas. The challenge became how to highlight that negative space without just quilting all straight lines. I treated each of the surrounding strips as a different section, mixing swirls and figure eights to differentiate one strip from the next. In the wreath centers, I quilted a feathery design that radiates from the center of each circle. It's a lot of variety, but the scrappy assortment of quilting designs ties in to the fabulous mix of scrappy fabrics!

SCRAPS GONE WILD

Safety First

SUSAN ACHE

QUILT SIZE: 60½" × 84½" | **BLOCK SIZE: 6" × 6"**

My original idea for this quilt was to use all bright colors and still have a red cross in the center. But I spend a lot of time searching for images of vintage quilts online, and the one thing they all have in common is the way the quilts have faded over time. Whether from real use or from being folded, the whites reveal differences with age, and the shades of colors change depending on where they are in the quilt. So I settled on using many different gray prints to achieve the washed-out look of a quilt that is kept in the car and taken to the beach. The bottom line—if you don't think of yourself as a scrappy quilter because a quilt of many colors isn't your jam, consider a multiple-fabric, but single-color-scheme quilt instead.

MATERIALS

Yardage is based on 42"-wide fabric. Fat eighths are 9" × 21".

- 30 fat eighths of assorted light prints for blocks
- 30 fat eighths of assorted gray prints for blocks
- ¼ yard of light print for plus-sign border
- ½ yard of red print for plus sign
- ⅓ yard of red tone on tone for plus-sign border
- ⅝ yard of dark gray print for binding
- 5⅛ yards of fabric for backing
- 67" × 91" piece of batting

CUTTING

All measurements include ¼" seam allowances.

From *each* light print fat eighth, cut:
3 strips, 2½" × 21" (90 total)

From *each* gray print fat eighth, cut:
3 strips, 2½" × 21" (90 total)

From the light print ¼-yard piece, cut:
4 strips, 1½" × 42"; crosscut into:
- 4 strips, 1½" × 12½"
- 4 strips, 1½" × 10½"
- 4 strips, 1½" × 6½"
- 4 pieces, 1½" × 3½"

From the red print, cut:
2 strips, 6½" × 42"; crosscut into:
- 3 pieces, 6½" × 12½"
- 2 pieces, 6½" × 9½"

From the red tone on tone, cut:
4 strips, 2½" × 42"; crosscut into:
- 8 strips, 2½" × 12½"
- 4 strips, 2½" × 10½"

From the dark gray print, cut:
8 strips, 2½" × 42"

MAKING THE BLOCKS

Press the seam allowances as indicated by the arrows.

1. Join one gray 2½" × 21" strip and two light 2½" × 21" strips to make strip set A, which should measure 6½" × 21", including seam allowances. Crosscut the strip set into six A segments, 2½" × 6½".

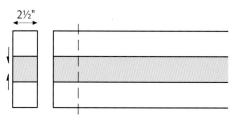

Make 1 A strip set, 6½" × 21".
Cut 6 A segments, 2½" × 6½".

2. Using the same prints as in step 1, join one light 2½" × 21" strip and two matching gray 2½" × 21" strips to make strip set B, which should measure 6½" × 21", including seam allowances. Crosscut the strip set into six B segments, 2½" × 6½".

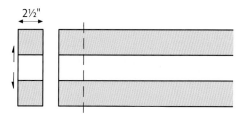

Make 1 B strip set, 6½" × 21".
Cut 6 B segments, 2½" × 6½".

3. Sew two A segments and one B segment together to make nine-patch block A. The block should measure 6½" square, including seam allowances. Repeat to make a second nine-patch block A.

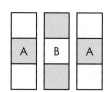

Make 2 of block A,
6½" × 6½".

MAKING THE CUT

To achieve my desired faded-over-time look, I started with all the prints, dots, and stripes shown below. In the end, the whites and creams worked best if they were really subtle and the grays were more or less blue-gray with no other colors in them. So the fabrics on the right went back into my stash to play with another day.

Too many colors.

Way too busy!

High contrast didn't look faded.

4. Sew two B segments and one A segment together to make nine-patch block B. The block should measure 6½" square, including seam allowances. Repeat to make a second nine-patch block B.

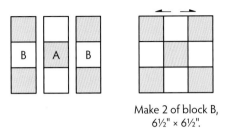

Make 2 of block B,
6½" × 6½".

5. Repeat steps 1–4 to make 30 sets total of two nine-patch A blocks and two nine-patch B blocks.

MAKING THE PLUS-SIGN UNITS

1. Sew a light print 1½" × 6½" strip to the left edge of a red print 6½" × 9½" piece. Refer to the diagram to add two red tone-on-tone 2½" × 10½" strips and two light print 1½" × 10½" strips. Sew a red tone-on-tone 2½" × 12½" strip to the left edge to make a side unit. Make two side units measuring 12½" square, including seam allowances.

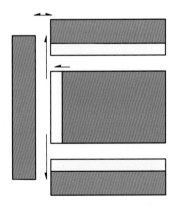

Make 2 units, 12½" × 12½".

2. Sew a light print 1½" × 12½" strip to one long edge of a remaining red tone-on-tone 2½" × 12½" strip. Make two. Sew a light print 1½" × 3½" piece to the top edge of each unit. Add a light print 1½" × 6½" strip to the bottom edge of a red print 6½" × 12½" piece. Join the three units in a horizontal row. Add a red tone-on-tone 2½" × 12½" strip to the bottom

edge to complete the unit. Make two top/bottom units measuring 12½" × 15½", including seam allowances.

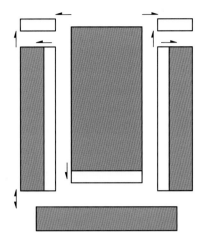

Make 2 units, 12½" × 15½".

ASSEMBLING THE QUILT TOP

Two each of nine-patch blocks A and B are sewn together in the final quilt to make 30 block units. Susan did not sew the blocks together until she actually started assembling the quilt top, allowing her to move the blocks around the quilt to create the washed-out look she was intending. If desired, follow Susan's example and wait to sew together the block units until after arranging them on a design wall.

1. Lay out two matching nine-patch A blocks and two matching nine-patch B blocks (from a different gray print) in two rows as shown, alternating A and B blocks. Sew together to make a block unit that measures 12½" square, including seam allowances. Make 30 block units.

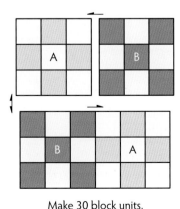

Make 30 block units,
12½" × 12½".

"While I imagined my quilt looking sun-faded from fun-filled days at the beach, it works great for indoor picnics too!" ~ Susan

2. Referring to the quilt assembly diagram, lay out the block units, plus-sign units, and remaining red print 6½" × 12½" piece in five columns. Sew together the pieces in each column. Join the columns to complete the quilt top, which should be 60½" × 84½".

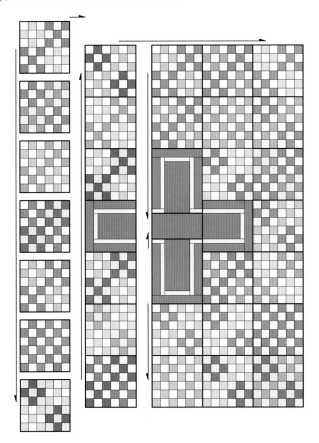

Quilting assembly

FINISHING THE QUILT

Go to ShopMartingale.com/HowtoQuilt to download free illustrated information if you need more details on any of the finishing steps.

1. Prepare the quilt backing so that it is about 6" larger in both directions than the quilt top.

2. Layer the backing, batting, and quilt top; baste the layers together.

3. Quilt by hand or machine. Susan's quilt is machine quilted with a combination of diagonal lines and waves in the gray nine-patch blocks. The large plus sign is quilted with a braid of diagonal lines in the red print and a meandering star in the red tone on tone.

4. Using the dark gray 2½"-wide strips, make the binding and attach it to the quilt.

Sue's Quilting Story

Knowing that Susan wanted to sew a new quilt that looked old, I opted for a quilting design that would create a lot of crinkly texture when the quilt was washed. You know—like an old quilt that has been well used, worn, loved and washed a lot that shows crinkles more than it shows a particular quilting motif. Of course, the red cross in the center needed its own special quilting design just to set it apart from the background. I stitched a herringbone type of pattern in each leg of the cross, all pointing toward the center.

Spooky Waves

SUSAN ACHE

QUILT SIZE: 84½" × 84½" | BLOCK SIZE: 8" × 8"

Haunted houses, costumes, candy, trick-or-treating . . . I love all things Halloween. (Did I mention the candy?) I particularly love this softer color palette featuring lighter oranges and charcoal grays rather than vibrant orange and inky black. Using the Cake Mix foundation patterns by Moda makes quick (and accurate) work of all those triangles, so don't be put off by them. Once you've pieced them, the real fun begins as you mix and match in this spin on an Ocean Waves quilt pattern. Speaking of fun, don't forget to reward yourself with your favorite fun-sized candies!

MATERIALS

Yardage is based on 42"-wide fabric. Susan used Moda Cake Mix Recipe papers to make the half-square-triangle units for her quilt. Cutting and assembly options are given for using the papers as well as for traditional methods.

If using Cake Mix papers:

• Cake Mix Recipe 3 (two packs)

• 54 squares, 10" × 10", plus 1⅝ yards *total* of assorted light prints for blocks and inner border

• 36 squares, 10" × 10", of assorted orange prints for blocks and inner border

• 18 squares, 10" × 10", of assorted black prints for blocks and inner border

If using traditional cutting method for half-square-triangle units:

• 5⅛ yards *total* of assorted light prints for blocks and inner border

• 2⅓ yards *total* of assorted orange prints for blocks and inner border

• 1¼ yards *total* of assorted black prints for blocks and inner border

For both methods:

• ⅜ yard of white print for middle border

• 2⅛ yards of orange floral for outer border and binding

• 7¾ yards of fabric for backing

• 93" × 93" piece of batting

CUTTING

All measurements include ¼" seam allowances. If you are using Cake Mix papers, don't cut any of the pieces marked with an asterisk (the 3" squares); you will use the uncut 10" squares to make the half-square-triangle units.

From the light prints, cut:

484 squares, 3" × 3"*
82 pieces, 2½" × 4½"
164 squares, 2½" × 2½"

From the orange prints, cut:

324 squares, 3" × 3"*

From the black prints, cut:

160 squares, 3" × 3"*

From the white print, cut:

8 strips, 1½" × 42"

From the orange floral, cut:

8 strips, 5½" × 42"
9 strips, 2½" × 42"

MAKING THE BLOCKS AND INNER-BORDER UNITS

Press all seam allowances as indicated by the arrows.

1. *If using Cake Mix papers:* Refer to the Cake Mix instructions to make 648 orange half-square-triangle units using 36 papers and 36 light print and 36 orange print 10" squares. Make 324 black triangle units (you will use only 320) using 18 papers and 18 light print and 18 dark print 10" squares.

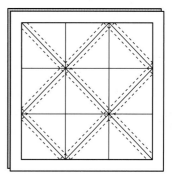

Make 648 units   Make 320 units
2½" × 2½".   2½" × 2½".

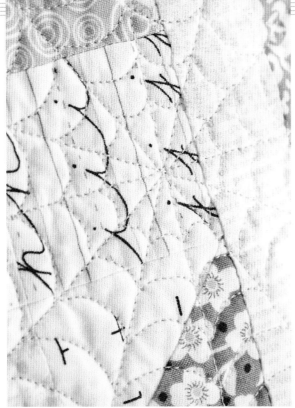

If using traditional sewing method: Use a pencil to mark a diagonal line from corner to corner on the wrong side of the light 3" squares. Layer a marked square on an orange square, right sides together. Sew ¼" from both sides of the drawn line. Cut the unit apart on the marked line to make two half-square-triangle units. Trim each unit to measure 2½" square, including seam allowances. Make 648 orange triangle units. Using black squares instead of orange print, repeat to make 320 black triangle units.

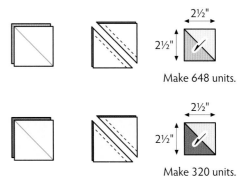

Make 648 units.

Make 320 units.

2. Lay out three orange triangle units, two black triangle units, one light 2½" square, and one light 2½" × 4½" piece in two rows as shown. Sew together the pieces in each row. Join the rows to make unit A, which should measure 4½" × 8½", including seam allowances. Make 72 of unit A.

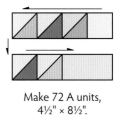

Make 72 A units,
4½" × 8½".

3. Using the same pieces but in a mirror-image arrangement, repeat step 2 to make unit B. Make eight of unit B.

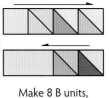

Make 8 B units,
4½" × 8½".

4. Lay out one light 2½" square, five orange triangle units, and two black triangle units in two rows as shown. Sew together the pieces in each row. Join the rows to make unit C, which should measure 4½" × 8½", including seam allowances. Make 72 of unit C.

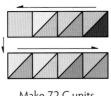

Make 72 C units,
4½" × 8½".

5. Using the same pieces but in a mirror-image arrangement, repeat step 4 to make unit D. Make eight of unit D.

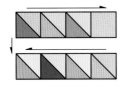

Make 8 D units,
4½" × 8½".

6. Lay out three orange triangle units and one light 2½" square in two rows as shown. Sew together the pieces in each row. Join the rows to make unit E, which should measure 4½" square, including seam allowances. Make two of unit E.

Make 2 E units,
4½" × 4½".

7. Sew a light 2½" square to one side of an orange triangle unit. Add a light 2½" × 4½" piece to the bottom edge to make unit F, which should measure 4½" square, including seam allowances. Make two of unit F.

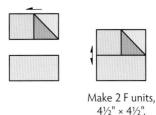

Make 2 F units,
4½" × 4½".

8. Rotating the units as shown, sew together one each of units A and C to make a block. Make 64 blocks, each 8½" square, including seam allowances. (Set the remaining units aside for making the inner pieced border.)

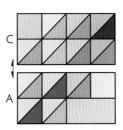

Make 64 blocks,
8½" × 8½".

Slow and Steady

I always take my time when sewing two sections together where points meet, such as the blocks in this quilt. There's nothing wrong with sewing slowly. Stitch to the intersection, lift the presser foot, and check to see if the needle is hitting both points as it should. It's also OK to redo a seam to make it right.

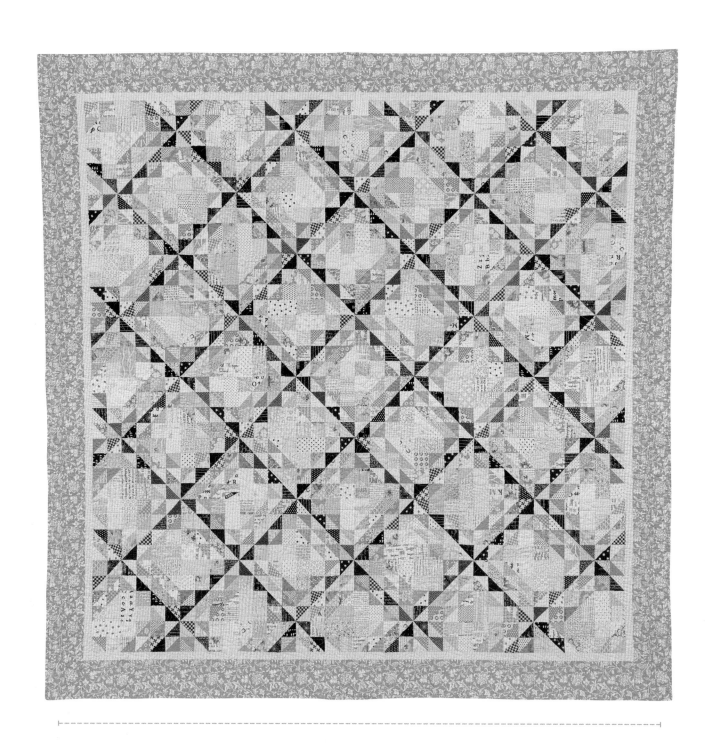

Designed and pieced by SUSAN ACHE; quilted by SUE ROGERS

ASSEMBLING THE QUILT CENTER

Lay out the blocks in eight rows of eight blocks each, rotating them as shown in the quilt assembly diagram. Sew together the blocks in each row. Join the rows to make the quilt center, which should be 64½" square, including seam allowances.

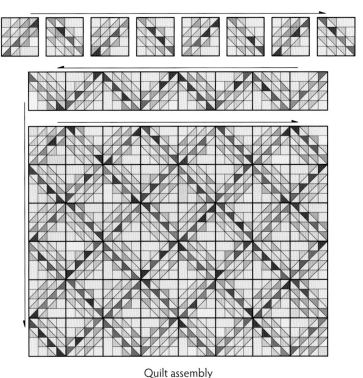

Quilt assembly

ASSEMBLING AND ADDING THE BORDERS

1. Sew together four each of units B and C, rotating them as shown, to make a border that measures 4½" × 64½", including seam allowances. Make two for the top and bottom inner borders.

Make 2 top/bottom borders, 4½" × 64½".

2. Sew together one each of units E and F and four each of units D and A, rotating them as shown, to make a border that measures 4½" × 72½", including seam allowances. Make two for the side inner borders.

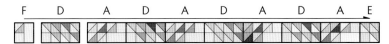

Make 2 side borders, 4½" × 72½".

Sue's Quilting Story

Having worked with Susan Ache for many years, both as a coworker at our local quilt shop and now as a client, I know how just how much she loves Halloween, including my spiderwebs pantograph pattern. Every now and then you'll find a spider stitched into the design (see photo above), so it also makes for a fun seek-and-find quilt. I've used this design on more than one of Susan's quilts, and I'm sure I'll use it again for her next spooktacular Halloween quilt design.

3. Referring to the diagram for adding borders, sew the pieced top/bottom inner-border strips to the top and bottom edges of the quilt top, rotating the bottom strip 180°. Add the pieced side inner-border strips to the remaining edges, rotating them as shown.

4. Join the white 1½" × 42" strips end to end and press the seam allowances open. Trim the pieced strip into two 74½"-long strips for the side middle borders and two 72½"-long strips for the top and bottom middle borders.

5. Sew the top and bottom middle-border strips to the top and bottom edges of the quilt top. Add the side middle-border strips to the remaining edges.

6. Join the orange 5½" × 42" strips end to end and press the seam allowances open. Trim the pieced strip into two 84½"-long strips for the side outer borders and two 74½"-long strips for the top and bottom outer borders.

7. Sew the top and bottom outer-border strips to the top and bottom edges of the quilt top. Add the side outer-border strips to the remaining edges to complete the quilt top, which should be 84½" square.

FINISHING THE QUILT

For more details on any of the finishing steps, go to ShopMartingale.com/HowtoQuilt to download free illustrated information.

1. Prepare the quilt backing so that it is about 8" larger in both directions than the quilt top.

2. Layer the backing, batting, and quilt top; baste the layers together.

3. Quilt by hand or machine. Susan's quilt is machine quilted with an allover spiderweb design.

4. Using the orange floral 2½"-wide strips, make the binding and attach it to the quilt.

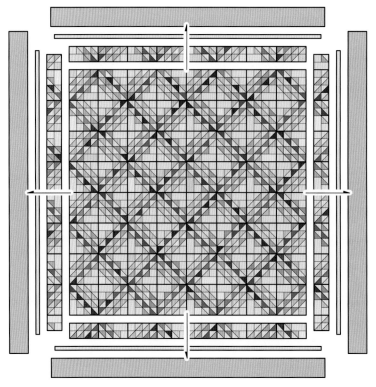

Adding the borders

"If making a scrappy quilt feels overwhelming, here's an easy plan. Choose one fabric of each color you want to use in the quilt. (I used orange, gray, and cream.) Lay out the three fabrics, repeating to pull other fabrics in each color, making sure to have an equal number of fabrics in each color. Take a picture on your phone and convert it to a black-and-white image. If anything jumps out like it doesn't belong, omit it!" ~Susan

A TALE OF TWO SEASONS

Mistletoe

LISSA ALEXANDER

QUILT SIZE: 72½" × 72½" | BLOCK SIZE: 12" × 12"

If Santa's making his list and checkin' it twice, I hope he leaves me a sleighful of red and green scraps under the tree and fills my stocking too! I'll use them all in a Christmastime quilt that has all the holiday feels without a scrap of novelty print in it . . . just a heaping helping of cozy holiday colors. Now, I know we're not supposed to play favorites, but I wanted the greens to be the stars of the quilt (you caught my eye and stole my heart, Mistletoe!), so I paired up with machine-quilter Maggi Honeyman to make them sparkle. Find her secret on page 103, and know that it's just between you and me!

MATERIALS

Yardage is based on 42"-wide fabric.

- 3⅞ yards *total* of assorted light prints for blocks
- 3⅛ yards *total* of assorted red prints for blocks
- 1⅛ yards *total* of assorted green prints for blocks
- ⅝ yard of white-and-green dot for binding
- 4½ yards of fabric for backing
- 81" × 81" piece of batting

CUTTING

All measurements include ¼" seam allowances.

From the light prints, cut:
18 squares, 7" × 7"; cut the squares in half diagonally
    to yield 36 large triangles
180 squares, 3" × 3"
288 squares, 2½" × 2½"

From the red prints, cut:
18 squares, 7" × 7"; cut the squares in half diagonally
    to yield 36 large triangles
180 squares, 3" × 3"
108 squares, 2⅞" × 2⅞"; cut the squares in half
    diagonally to yield 216 small triangles

From the green prints, cut:
216 squares, 2½" × 2½"

From the white-and-green dot, cut:
8 strips, 2½" × 42"

MAKING THE BLOCKS

Press all seam allowances as indicated by the arrows.

1. Use a pencil to mark a diagonal line from corner to corner on the wrong side of the light 3" squares. Layer a marked square on a red square, right sides together. Sew ¼" from both sides of the drawn line. Cut the unit apart on the marked line to make two half-square-triangle units. Square up and trim each unit to measure 2½" square, including seam allowances. Make 360 half-square-triangle units.

Make 360 units.

2. Lay out three red small triangles, two light 2½" squares, and one half-square-triangle unit in three rows. Sew the pieces into rows. Join the rows. Make 72 pieced triangle units.

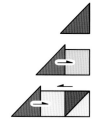 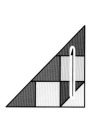

Make 72 units.

3. Sew a light large triangle to the diagonal edge of a pieced triangle unit to make unit A. Trim and square up the unit to measure 6½" square, including seam allowances. Make 36 of unit A.

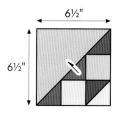

Make 36 A units.

4. Using red large triangles instead of light print, repeat step 3 to make 36 of unit B.

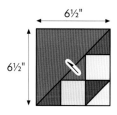

Make 36 B units.

5. Lay out two light 2½" squares, four half-square-triangle units, and three green 2½" squares in three rows of three. Sew the pieces into rows. Join the rows to make unit C, which should measure 6½" square, including seam allowances. Make 72 of unit C.

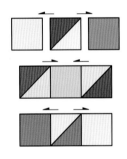
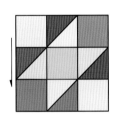

Make 72 C units,
6½" × 6½".

6. Arrange one each of units A and B and two of unit C in two rows as shown, rotating units so seams abut. Join the units in rows. Sew the rows together to make a block measuring 12½" square, including seam allowances. Make 36 blocks.

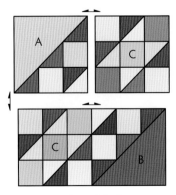

Make 36 blocks,
12½" × 12½".

Custom Quilting

When is custom quilting the right options versus edge-to-edge quilting? Machine quilter Maggi Honeyman shares her thoughts:

"Quilters' perception of machine quilting has changed greatly over the years. I do edge-to-edge designs on so many more quilts today than I ever did years ago. Sometimes a quilter chooses custom quilting for a special occasion quilt, such as a wedding or anniversary. Sometimes it comes down to budget, because custom work does make a difference in cost. I think if a quilter feels like she's invested her best effort in making a quilt, or considers it a lifetime achievement, then it deserves custom quilting. It's worth it to save up to have it custom quilted. It also doesn't mean you have to do heirloom quilting. There are degrees of simplicity in custom quilting too, if you don't want something too heavily quilted."

MAKING THE CUT

Even though I work for Moda Fabrics and we produce many beautiful Christmas prints each year, I challenged myself to make a holiday quilt with not a "Christmas print" in sight. Why limit yourself to *Christmas green?* Using all the shades adds just the right amount of sparkle!

Designed and pieced by **LISSA ALEXANDER**; quilted by **MAGGI HONEYMAN**

ASSEMBLING THE QUILT TOP

Lay out the blocks in six rows of six, rotating them as shown in the quilt assembly diagram. Sew together the blocks in each row. Join the rows to complete the quilt top, which should be 72½" square.

Quilt assembly

FINISHING THE QUILT

Go to ShopMartingale.com/HowtoQuilt to download free illustrated information if you need more details on any of the finishing steps.

1. Prepare the quilt backing so that it is about 8" larger in both directions than the quilt top.

2. Layer the backing, batting, and quilt top; baste the layers together.

3. Quilt by hand or machine. Lissa's quilt is machine quilted with a feathered square in the hourglass units formed at each intersection of four blocks. Diagonal lines run through the center of each white square and the half-square-triangle units. Each green square is filled with a grouping of four quilted leaves.

4. Using the white-and-green dot 2½"-wide strips, make the binding and attach it to the quilt.

Maggi's Quilting Notes

Lissa had a vision dancing in her head when it came to this holiday beauty. Even though the quilt top reads as a red quilt with green accents, she wanted the greens to be the sparklers. To make her vision come to life, I did custom quilting using cream-colored thread. I chose fairly simple straight line stitching through the small squares and half-square-triangles. Nothing too fancy. Then I added the curvy four-petal motifs to each green square, drawing more attention to them. But, because balance is also important, I added a second soft element by quilting a feathery wreath in the center of each red square where the blocks meet.

Garden Path

LISSA ALEXANDER

QUILT SIZE: 69½" × 86½" | BLOCK SIZE: 9" × 9"

More often than not, what catches my eye with a quilt pattern is when a secondary pattern emerges that makes me question where the blocks begin and end and how it is constructed. It's like unlocking a little mystery. For Garden Path, what do you see? Giant green stars that look a little groovy? Or plus-sign blocks with nine-patches in the corners? The blocks and the stars that capture most of the attention are actually formed secondarily by the sashing as you join the quilt top pieces. Have fun watching the bursting stars emerge as you combine the elements in this two-for-one design!

MATERIALS

Yardage is based on 42"-wide fabric.

- ¼ yard *total* of assorted red prints for nine-patch centers
- 1¼ yards *total* of assorted blue, aqua, orange, yellow, green, and pink prints (collectively referred to as "bright" throughout) for nine-patch units
- 2⅓ yards of green solid for sashing, inner border, and binding
- 4½ yards of white dot for blocks, sashing, setting triangles, and outer border
- 5⅓ yards of fabric for backing
- 78" × 95" piece of batting
- Template plastic

CUTTING

All measurements include ¼" seam allowances. Trace patterns A and B on page 112 onto template plastic and cut out on the drawn lines. Trace the templates onto the wrong side of the 5"-wide strips as specified below, rotating the templates 180° after each cut to make the best use of your fabric.

From the assorted red prints, cut:
82 squares, 1½" × 1½"

From the bright prints, cut:
656 squares, 1½" × 1½"

From the green solid, cut:
6 strips, 5" × 42"; crosscut into 96 *each* of triangle A and A reversed
15 strips, 2½" × 42"
4 strips, 2" × 42"; crosscut into 72 squares, 2" × 2"

From the white dot, cut:
8 strips, 7½" × 42"
1 strip, 6¾" × 42"; crosscut into 3 squares, 6¾" × 6¾". Cut the squares into quarters diagonally to yield 12 medium triangles (2 will be extra).
6 strips, 5" × 42"; crosscut into 96 of triangle B
2 strips, 4" × 42"; crosscut into 7 strips, 4" × 10"
12 strips, 3½" × 42"; crosscut into:
- 17 strips, 3½" × 9½"
- 14 pieces, 3½" × 7"
- 54 squares, 3½" × 3½". Cut *2 of the squares* in half diagonally to yield 4 small triangles.

MAKING THE BLOCKS AND SASHING UNITS

Press the seam allowances in the directions indicated by the arrows.

1. Lay out eight bright print 1½" squares and one red print 1½" square in three rows as shown. Sew together the squares in each row. Join the rows to make a nine-patch unit that measures 3½" square, including seam allowances. Repeat to make 82 nine-patch units.

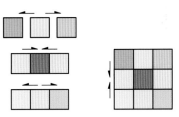

Make 82 nine-patch units, 3½" × 3½".

2. Use a pencil to mark a diagonal line on the wrong side of each green 2" square. Align a marked square right side down on one corner of a white 3½" square as shown. Sew on the drawn line. Trim the seam allowances to ¼" and press the resulting triangle toward the corner. Add three more marked squares in the same manner to make a square-in-a-square unit that measures 3½" square, including seam allowances. Make 18 units total.

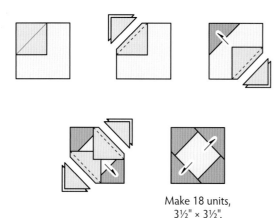

Make 18 units,
3½" × 3½".

3. Sew a green A triangle to one edge of a white B triangle; be sure the blunt tip of the B triangle is pointing up. Add a green A reversed triangle to the adjacent edge of the B triangle as shown. The unit should measure 3½" × 5", including seam allowances. Make 96 units.

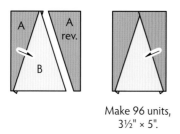

Make 96 units,
3½" × 5".

4. Sew together two units from step 3 as shown to make a sashing unit that measures 3½" × 9½", including seam allowances. Make 48 sashing units.

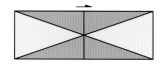

Make 48 units, 3½" × 9½".

5. Lay out four nine-patch units, two white 3½" squares, and one white 3½" × 9½" strip in three rows as shown. Sew together the pieces in each row. Join

the rows to make a block that measures 9½" square, including seam allowances. Make 17 blocks.

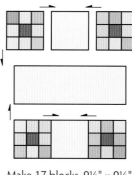

Make 17 blocks, 9½" × 9½".

MAKING THE SETTING UNITS

1. Lay out two white 3½" × 7" pieces, two nine-patch units, and one white 4" × 10" strip in three rows as shown. Sew together the pieces in each row. Join the rows to make a setting unit that measures 10" square, including seam allowances. Make seven setting units.

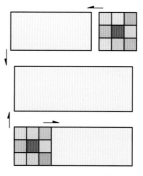

Make 7 setting units, 10" × 10".

2. Cut each setting unit in half diagonally as shown to make 14 pieced setting triangles. The edges of the pieced setting triangles will be on the bias, so handle them carefully.

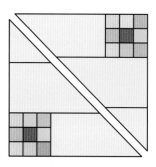

Cut into 14 setting triangles.

ASSEMBLING THE QUILT CENTER

1. Referring to the quilt assembly diagram, lay out the blocks, pieced setting triangles, sashing units, square-in-a-square units, and white medium triangles in 13 diagonal rows. Sew together the pieces in each row. Join the rows, and then add the white small triangles to the corners to complete the quilt center.

Quilt assembly

2. Trim the quilt center, leaving ¼" beyond the points of the sashing rectangles. The quilt center should measure 51½" × 68½", including seam allowances.

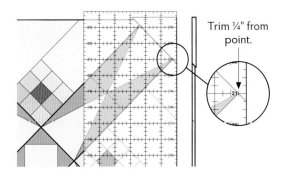

Trim ¼" from point.

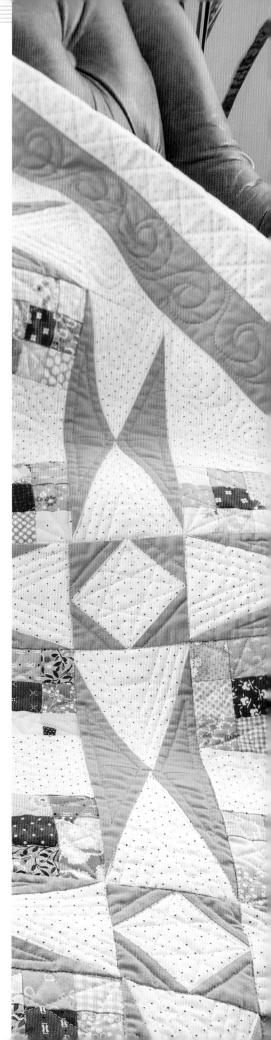

Designed and pieced by LISSA ALEXANDER; quilted by MAGGI HONEYMAN

ADDING THE BORDERS

1. Join seven of the green 2½" × 42" strips end to end and press the seam allowances open. Trim the pieced strip into two 51½"-long strips for the top and bottom inner borders and two 72½"-long strips for the side inner borders. Sew the top and bottom inner-border strips to the quilt top and then add the side inner-border strips. The quilt top should measure 55½" × 72½", including seam allowances.

2. Join the white 7½" × 42" strips end to end and press the seam allowances open. Trim the pieced strip into two 55½"-long strips for the top and bottom outer borders and two 86½"-long strips for the side outer borders. Sew the top and bottom outer-border strips to the quilt top and then add the side outer-border strips. The completed quilt top should be 69½" × 86½".

Adding borders

Maggi's Quilting Notes

When you step up close, you can see that the blocks in this quilt have a nine-patch in each corner. My goal was to play up the sashing stars created by the secondary design. Straight line quilting accentuates the strong angle of those pieces and highlights their shapes with echo quilting in the light areas. Because I feel strongly that elements across the quilt top need to relate to one another, I quilted the center of the sashing stars and the nine-patches in the same way—corner, center, corner, center, corner, center, corner, center—to make an eight-pointed star with the quilting. The plus signs in the blocks have swirling circles to contrast with the sharp angles used everywhere else. And good old crosshatching in the borders finishes the look with a traditional flair.

FINISHING THE QUILT

For more details on any of the finishing steps, go to ShopMartingale.com/HowtoQuilt to download free illustrated information.

1. Prepare the quilt backing so that it is about 8" larger in both directions than the quilt top.

2. Layer the backing, batting, and quilt top; baste the layers together.

3. Quilt by hand or machine. Lissa's quilt is machine quilted with an eight-pointed star in each nine-patch unit, an overall spiral in the white areas of the blocks and pieced setting triangles, and echoed triangles in the sashing. The inner border has a continuous swirl and the outer border has diagonal crosshatching.

4. Using the remaining green solid 2½"-wide strips, make the binding and attach it to the quilt.

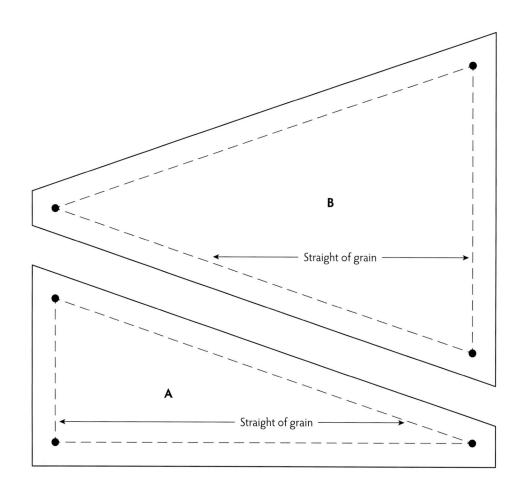

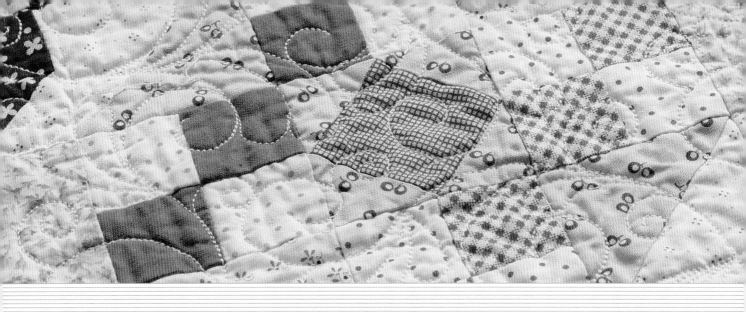

I'LL HAVE SECONDS

Roundel

SUSAN ACHE

QUILT SIZE: 83" × 83" | BLOCK SIZE: 7½" × 7½"

How many different ways can you say "medallion"? Apparently a ton, according to the dictionary, and one of them is the cute word that I landed on for this project's name. There's something so appealing to me about a medallion quilt, and I thought it would be fun to construct one without the round-and-round part of it. Instead, I designed this quilt to be made in sections and rows. You can make the individual parts ahead of time and put them in piles to be arranged at a later date. If you don't have a design wall, don't worry. You can still work this quilt in sections—just pay attention to the orientation of the blocks when it's time for final assembly.

MATERIALS

Yardage is based on 42"-wide fabric. Fat quarters are 18" × 21"; fat eighths are 9" × 21".

- ⅔ yard of white-and-blue dot for blocks and units
- 1½ yards of red solid for blocks, units, and border
- 1 yard of white-and-red dot for blocks and units
- 1⅝ yards of red check for blocks, units, and binding
- 2⅝ yards of white print for blocks and units
- 13 fat quarters of assorted blue prints for blocks and units
- ⅝ yard of pink print for blocks and units
- 16 fat eighths of assorted red prints for units
- ½ yard of white-and-red print for blocks and units
- ⅞ yard of light blue floral for blocks and units
- ⅓ yard of white-and-red floral for blocks and units
- 7⅝ yards of fabric for backing
- 91" × 91" piece of batting

CUTTING

All measurements include ¼" seam allowances.

From the white-and-blue dot, cut:
12 strips, 1¾" × 42"; crosscut *1 of the strips* into
    16 squares, 1¾" × 1¾"

From the red solid, cut:
10 strips, 3" × 42"; crosscut *1 of the strips* into
    8 squares, 3" × 3"
11 strips, 1¾" × 42"

From the white-and-red dot, cut:
18 strips, 1¾" × 42"; crosscut *7 of the strips* into
    136 squares, 1¾" × 1¾"

From the red check, cut:
3 strips, 3" × 42"; crosscut into 36 squares, 3" × 3"
9 strips, 2½" × 42"
11 strips, 1¾" × 42"

From the pink print, cut:
3 strips, 3½" × 42"; crosscut into 30 squares,
    3½" × 3½"
5 strips, 1¾" × 42"; crosscut into 96 squares,
    1¾" × 1¾"

From the white print, cut:
9 strips, 3½" × 42"; crosscut into 96 squares,
    3½" × 3½"
30 strips, 1¾" × 42"; crosscut into:
- 232 pieces, 1¾" × 3"
- 256 squares, 1¾" × 1¾"

From *each* blue print fat quarter, cut:
1 strip, 3½" × 21"; crosscut into 4 squares, 3½" × 3½"
    (52 total; 2 are extra)
1 strip, 3" × 21"; crosscut into 4 squares, 3" × 3"
    (52 total; 3 are extra)
2 strips, 1¾" × 21"; crosscut into 16 squares, 1¾" × 1¾"
    (208 total; 8 are extra)

From scraps of assorted blue prints, cut 16 sets of:
1 square, 3½" × 3½"
2 squares, 1¾" × 1¾"

From *each* red print fat eighth, cut:
2 strips, 3½" × 21" (32 total); crosscut into 16 pieces,
    1¾" × 3½" (256 total)

From the white-and-red print, cut:
5 strips, 3" × 42"; crosscut into 64 squares, 3" × 3"

From the light blue floral, cut:
9 strips, 3" × 42"; crosscut into 112 squares, 3" × 3"

From the white-and-red check, cut:
3 strips, 3" × 42"; crosscut into 32 squares, 3" × 3"

MAKING THE BLOCK UNITS

Press the seam allowances as indicated by the arrows.

1. Join one white-and-blue dot and one red solid 1¾" × 42" strip to make strip set A, which should measure 3" × 42", including seam allowances. Make 11 of strip set A. Crosscut the strip sets into 224 A segments, 1¾" × 3".

Make 11 A strip sets, 3" × 42".
Cut 224 A segments, 1¾" × 3".

Designed and pieced by **SUSAN ACHE**; quilted by **SUE ROGERS**

2. Sew together two A segments, positioning them as shown, to make an A unit that is 3" square, including seam allowances. Make 112 A units.

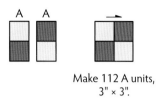

Make 112 A units,
3" × 3".

3. Join one white-and-red dot and one red check 1¾" × 42" strip to make strip set B, which should measure 3" × 42", including seam allowances. Make 11 of strip set B. Crosscut the strip sets into 224 B segments, 1¾" × 3".

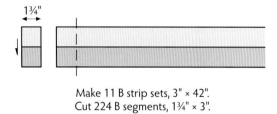

Make 11 B strip sets, 3" × 42".
Cut 224 B segments, 1¾" × 3".

4. Sew together two B segments, rotating one segment as shown, to make a B unit that measures 3" square, including seam allowances. Make 112 B units.

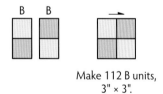

Make 112 B units,
3" × 3".

5. Use a pencil to mark a diagonal line from corner to corner on the wrong side of each white print 3½" square. Layer a marked square on a pink print 3½" square, right sides together. Sew ¼" from both sides of the drawn line. Cut the unit apart on the marked line to make two half-square-triangle units. Trim each

unit to measure 3" square, including seam allowances. Make 60 C units.

Make 60 C units.

6. Using the remaining marked white print 3½" squares and the assorted blue print 3½" squares, repeat step 5 to make 132 half-square-triangle D units, each 3" square, including seam allowances. You should have 25 sets of four matching half-square-triangle units and 16 sets of two matching half-square-triangle units.

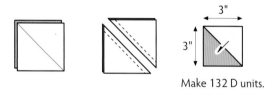

Make 132 D units.

7. Use a pencil to mark a diagonal line on the wrong side of each pink print 1¾" square. Set aside two 3" squares from each blue print (26 total) for "Making the Blocks" on page 119. On a remaining blue print 3" square, align a marked pink square right side down on one corner as shown. Sew on the drawn line. Trim the seam allowances to ¼" and press the resulting triangle toward the corner. Add three more marked pink squares in the same manner to make an E unit that measures 3" square, including seam allowances. Make 24 E units total.

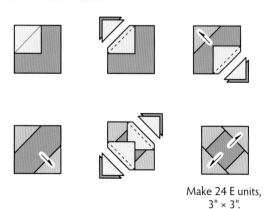

Make 24 E units,
3" × 3".

8. Use a pencil to mark a diagonal line on the wrong side of 128 white-and-red dot 1¾" squares. Using the marked squares and red check 3" squares, repeat step 7 to make 32 F units total.

Make 32 F units,
3" × 3".

9. Use a pencil to mark a diagonal line on the wrong side of each white-and-blue dot 1¾" square. Align a marked square right side down on one corner of a red solid 3" square as shown. Sew on the drawn line. Trim the seam allowances to ¼" and press the resulting triangle toward the corner. Add a second marked square in the same manner to make a G unit that measures 3" square, including seam allowances. Make eight G units total.

Make 8 G units,
3" × 3".

10. Mark a diagonal line on the wrong side of each remaining white-and-red dot 1¾" square. Using the marked squares and red check 3" squares, repeat step 9 to make four H units total.

Make 4 H units,
3" × 3".

11. Mark a diagonal line on the wrong side of each blue print 1¾" square. Align a marked square right side down on one end of a white print 1¾" × 3" piece

as shown. Sew on the drawn line. Trim the seam allowances to ¼" and press the resulting triangle toward the corner. Add a second marked square on the opposite end of the white piece to make an I unit, which should measure 1¾" × 3", including seam allowances. Make 116 I units total (25 sets of four matching units plus 16 single units).

Make 116 I units,
1¾" × 3".

12. Mark a diagonal line on the wrong side of each white print 1¾" square. Using the marked squares and red print 1¾" × 3" pieces, repeat step 11 to make 128 J units (32 sets of four matching units).

Make 128 J units,
1¾" × 3".

MAKING THE BLOCKS

1. Lay out the following in three rows, rotating them as shown: two each of units A, B, and C; one unit E; and two white-and-red print 3" squares. Sew together the pieces in each row. Join the rows to make a multicolored block that measures 8" square, including seam allowances. Make 20 multicolored blocks.

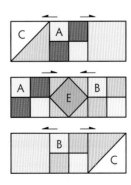 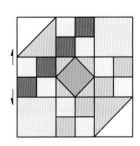

Make 20 multicolored blocks,
8" × 8".

2. Lay out the following in three rows, rotating them as shown: two each of units A and C; one each of units E, G, and H; and two white-and-red print 3" squares. Sew together the pieces in each row. Join the rows to make an inner-point block that measures 8" square, including seam allowances. Make four inner point blocks.

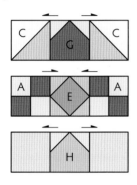 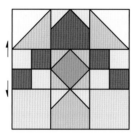

Make 4 inner-point blocks,
8" × 8".

3. Lay out the following in two rows, rotating them as shown: two white-and-red print 3" squares, one unit G, two of unit A, and one light blue floral 3" square. Sew together the pieces in each row. Join the rows to make an outer-point block that measures 8" × 5½", including seam allowances. Make four outer-point blocks.

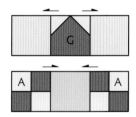 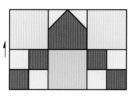

Make 4 outer-point blocks,
8" × 5½".

4. Join a unit I with a white print 1¾" × 3" piece to make a blue side unit that is 3" square, including seam allowances. Make 116 blue side units total (25 sets of four matching units plus 16 single units).

Make 116 side units,
3" × 3".

5. Matching the blue print in all units and pieces, lay out four of unit D, four blue side units, and one blue print 3" square in three rows. Sew together the pieces in each row. Join the rows to make a blue block that measures 8" square, including seam allowances. Make 25 blue blocks.

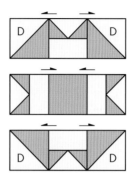 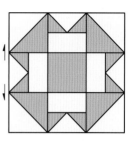

Make 25 blue blocks,
8" × 8".

6. Matching the blue print in all units and pieces, sew together two of unit D and one blue side unit to make a partial blue block. The block should be 8" × 3", including seam allowances. Make 16 partial blue blocks.

Make 16 partial blue blocks,
8" × 3".

7. Matching the red print in all units and pieces, join a unit J with a red print 1¾" × 3" piece to make a red side unit that measures 3" square, including seam allowances. Make 128 red side units total (32 sets of four matching units).

Make 128 red side units,
3" × 3".

What kind of quilts would you be making if you let go of the limitations you've set for yourself? Instead of telling yourself you're not good at something, assume you're going to be great at it and have a little more fun! Quilting should be easy and playful, not stressful. Enjoy the process! ~ Lissa

ASSEMBLING THE QUILT TOP

Take a look at the quilt assembly diagrams below and on page 124 before you start laying out the quilt top. The quilt top is assembled in four large corner sections and four side sections, all surrounding the center blue block. The red side units; all remaining A, B, C, and F units; and all remaining 3" squares will be used as sashing pieces around the blocks. If possible, lay out the entire quilt on a design wall, placing each set of four matching red side units as shown to form a "block" in the finished quilt top. If it's not possible for you to lay out the entire quilt, work on one corner section and one side section at a time, remembering to match the red side units on adjacent sections.

1. For each corner section, lay out five multicolored blocks, four blue blocks, and four blue partial blocks, leaving room in between for the sashing. Then arrange a set of matching red side units and a unit F at the intersection of each block. Finally, arrange the following pieces and units to form the remainder of the sashing: 14 of unit A, 16 of unit B, three of unit C, two white-and-red print 3" squares, 24 light blue floral 3" squares, and eight white-and-red floral 3" squares.

2. Sew together the pieces in each sashing rectangle (each group of three units or 3" squares) and press as shown. Then sew together the pieces in each horizontal row; press the seam allowances away from each sashing rectangle. Join the rows to make a corner section; press the seam allowances toward the sashing rows. The corner section should be 35½" square, including seam allowances. Make four corner sections.

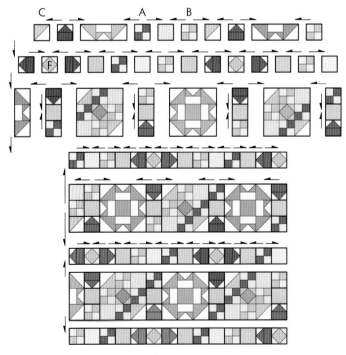

Make 4 corner sections, 35½" × 35½".

Sue's Quilting Story

Arranged with a center medallion but pieced in blocks, rows, and sections rather than in rounds, Roundel offers so much visual interest to keep your eyes moving across the quilt top. To avoid competing with the design and to add some counterpoint to all the squares, rectangles, and points, I opted for an allover swirling design to soften things up a bit. And, while Susan generally doesn't like quilt borders to be quilted differently than the rest of the quilt, in this case the solid red border clearly makes a final statement to the quilt design, so I felt it needed its own design. Again, I chose a curvy design to keep your eyes flowing around the edges.

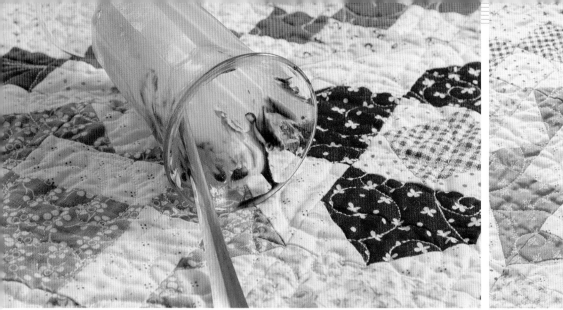

3. For each side section, lay out one outer-point block, two blue blocks, and one inner-point block, leaving room in between for the sashing. Arrange four red side units, three light blue floral 3" squares, and two of unit B to form the sashing. Sew together the pieces in each sashing rectangle (each group of three units or 3" squares) and press as shown. Join the blocks and sashing rectangles to make a side section. Press the seam allowances away from the sashing rectangles.

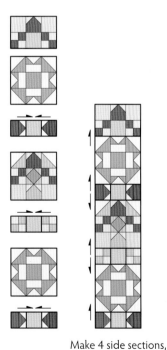

Make 4 side sections,
8" × 35½".

4. Lay out the corner sections, side sections, and remaining blue block in three rows. Sew together the pieces in each row. Join the rows to make the quilt center, which should measure 78" square, including seam allowances.

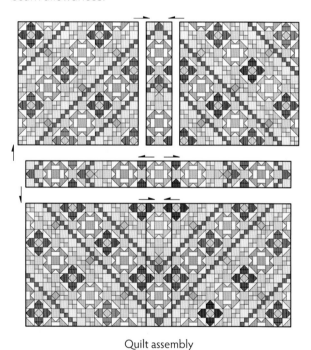

Quilt assembly

ADDING THE BORDER

1. Join the red solid 3" × 42" strips end to end and press the seam allowances open. Trim the pieced strip into two 78"-long strips for the side borders and two 83"-long strips for the top and bottom borders.

2. Sew the side border strips to opposite edges of the quilt top. Add the top and bottom border strips to the remaining edges to complete the quilt top, which should be 83" square.

FINISHING THE QUILT

For more details on any of the finishing steps, go to ShopMartingale.com/HowtoQuilt to download free illustrated information.

1. Prepare the quilt backing so that it is about 8" larger in both directions than the quilt top.

2. Layer the backing, batting, and quilt top; baste the layers together.

3. Quilt by hand or machine. Susan's quilt is machine quilted with an allover feather-and-spiral design in the quilt center. The border has a feathered design with spirals in the corners.

4. Using the red check 2½"-wide strips, make the binding and attach it to the quilt.

Picture This

When you are making the quilt, it's very helpful to take pictures along the way before you actually do your sewing. (Ask me how I know!) Even though these are fairly simple shapes, they can be turned easily and you may not notice until you've sewn them into place. Take a picture with the setting complete and look closely at your layout to make sure everything is turned in the correct direction.

Adding the borders

A Big Finish

Once the quilt top is done, there's still more fun ahead! Professional long-arm quilters Maggi Honeyman and Sue Rogers share a few pro tips to make sure your finish is as strong as your start.

Choosing a thread color for quilting

"When I step back from a quilt top, a light thread color blends better on a dark fabric than a dark thread blends on a light fabric. For that reason, on a scrappy quilt I most often choose lighter thread colors. My most used thread is Omni by Superior Thread." (Tex 30/40 wt.) –Maggi

"I spread out a quilt on a table to choose a thread color. I usually opt for a grayed-down color so it doesn't stand out too much. I like Superior Threads because they're so fine they sink into the fabric, helping you notice the quilting design more than the thread color." –Sue

Batting preferences

"My go-to battings are both from Moda: Luna Loft (80 cotton/20 poly) and Kyoto Bamboo Blend (50 bamboo/50 cotton)." –Maggi

"My preferred battings are Quilters Dream Cotton Request (the thinnest of their cottons) and Quilters Dream Bamboo and Silk." –Sue

Pressing matters

"Pressing is huge. After you press your quilt top from the back, turn it over and press it again from the right side." –Maggi

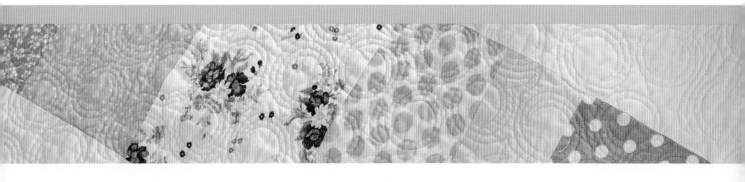

Thoughts on scale

"The scale of the quilting should be proportionate to the size of the patchwork pieces. Teeny tiny pieces need more dense quilting because more pieces need to be hit with the quilting stitches." –Maggi

"Elaborate designs don't show up well on busy quilts, so I'll choose an overall design that pairs well with a quilt's theme. I think of the quilting as the background singer (unless there are big open areas that deserve to showcase custom-quilted feathers or the like). I also prefer quilting to be evenly distributed across the quilt top, so you don't end up with flat areas filled with dense quilting and puffy areas where there's barely any quilting." –Sue

The number one mistake quilters make

"Your quilt backing needs to be squared up. If you sew two pieces of fabric together, one can't be 6" longer than the other—the quilt won't load properly on the long arm. And when you're cutting, remember to use scissors or a rotary blade that's sharp so the fabric edges are clean. Finally, if you have a specific direction you want the backing to run, mark the top of your quilt top and the top of your backing." –Maggi

"When piecing a quilt backing, the edges all need to be even. If they're not, your quilter can't properly load the quilt on the long arm. And the fabric needs to be cut on the fabric grain. If it's not cut on the grain, the completed quilt won't hang or drape nicely." –Sue

About the Authors

LISSA ALEXANDER

I've had a crazy, amazing life, a wild journey that I could never have imagined. Through it all, I've learned to take the pieces and stitch them together to make something new. My life is a patchwork of family, friends, and people who have made an impact.

The first quilt I made was one my sister and I worked on together—a quilt-as-you go quilt for a wedding gift. My next quilt was made from a sampler pack of a thousand 1½" squares. (Clearly I was destined to become a scrap quilter, although I thought the finished quilt would be bigger.)

The rest of my story is still a work in progress. That first wedding quilt led to working in a quilt shop. I raised kids and now I'm blessed with grandchildren. I'm part of an industry and community of people who share my love for quilts and the people who make them.

To everyone reading this . . . thank you for being part of my scrappy story.

Instagram: @modalissa | Blog: Modalissa.com

SUSAN ACHE

All I ever wanted to know about quilting was how to make a Nine Patch block so I could feature my love of embroidery. Ha! After I made my first quilt, I realized quilting had opened up a whole new world to this mom of five (now grown) children. I turned many hours of reading about quiltmaking into a lifelong passion for creating beautiful quilts.

I'm often asked where I find inspiration. Color inspiration often comes from my native Florida surroundings, and I love nothing more than finding fun new ways to show off as many colors as I can in a quilt. My favorite part of the journey is simply making a plan and then stitching blocks. I could sew blocks all day long!

Working in a quilt store for years helped cultivate my love of color and fabric. With so many fabric options out there, I don't see my creative journey ending for a long time.

Instagram: @yardgrl60